It Makes Sense!

Using Ten-Frames to Build Number Sense

Grades K–2

Melissa Conklin

Math Solutions
Sausalito, California, USA

Math Solutions
One Harbor Drive, Suite 101
Sausalito, CA 94965
www.mathsolutions.com

Library of Congress Cataloging-in-Publication Data
Conklin, Melissa.
  It makes sense!: using ten-frames to build number sense grades k-2 / Melissa Conklin.
    p. cm.
  Includes bibliographical references and index.
  Summary: "Ten-frames are a model to help students efficiently gain and develop an understanding of addition and subtraction. The classroom-tested routines, games, and problem-solving lessons in this book use ten-frames to develop students' natural strategies for adding numbers and fit into any set of state standards or curriculum"—Provided by publisher.
  ISBN 978-1-935099-10-9 (alk. paper)
1. Mathematics—Study and teaching (Early childhood) 2. Mathematics—Study and teaching (Elementary) 3. Early childhood education. 4. Concept learning. I. Title.
  QA135.6.C658 2010
  372.7'2—dc22   2010002038

Editor: Jamie Ann Cross
Production: Melissa L. Inglis-Elliott
Cover & interior design: Susan Barclay/Barclay Design
Composition: Macmillan Publishing Solutions

Cover photo: Erin Keenan's kindergarten class at South Shades Crest Elementary School, Hoover, Alabama. Videographer: Friday's Films, www.fridaysfilms.com

Printed in the United States of America on acid-free paper

15 14 13 12 ML   3 4 5

A Message from Math Solutions

We at Math Solutions believe that teaching math well calls for increasing our understanding of the math we teach, seeking deeper insights into how students learn mathematics, and refining our lessons to best promote students' learning.

Math Solutions shares classroom-tested lessons and teaching expertise from our faculty of professional development consultants as well as from other respected math educators. Our publications are part of the nationwide effort we've made since 1984 that now includes

- more than five hundred face-to-face professional development programs each year for teachers and administrators in districts across the country;
- professional development books that span all math topics taught in kindergarten through high school;
- videos for teachers and for parents that show math lessons taught in actual classrooms;
- on-site visits to schools to help refine teaching strategies and assess student learning; and
- free online support, including grade-level lessons, book reviews, inservice information, and district feedback, all in our Math Solutions Online Newsletter.

For information about all of the products and services we have available, please visit our website at *www.mathsolutions.com*. You can also contact us to discuss math professional development needs by calling (800) 868-9092 or by sending an email to *info@mathsolutions.com*.

We're always eager for your feedback and interested in learning about your particular needs. We look forward to hearing from you.

FOUNDED BY MARILYN BURNS

Contents

SECTION III: Problem-Solving Lessons Using Ten-Frames

Reproducibles

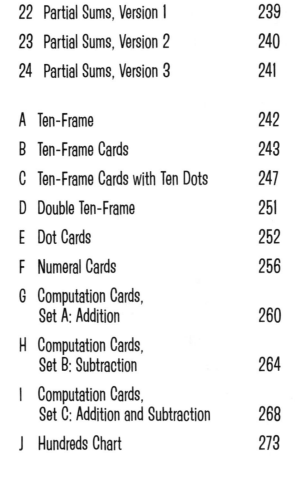

Assessments

Teacher Reflections

Acknowledgments

It is not knowledge but the act of learning, not possession but the act of getting there, which grants the greatest enjoyment . . .

Karl Freidrich Gauss, *Letter to Bolyai*

I am forever indebted to my many colleagues at Math Solutions who have shaped, guided, and fostered my learning and teaching of mathematics as well as my endeavor to become the author of this book: Stephanie Sheffield, my mentor, math coach, and friend, who was and is patient, insightful, and encouraging; Jamie Cross, who answered every question with joy in her voice and cheered me on from the very beginning; Melissa Inglis-Elliott, whose expertise made the production of this book possible; Linda Honeyman, my content editor, who walked through each chapter with me and asked all the right questions to help make this book the best it could be; Chris Brunette, who acted as a sounding board for me when I had ideas or questions; and Lu Ann Weynand, my colleague and retreat roommate, who always has an open ear and knows just what to say. And finally, Marilyn Burns: It is her vision and dedication that has made immeasurable impact on math education.

I would like to thank the following principals and teachers for allowing me to work at their schools and with their students. At Brandenburg Elementary in Irving, Texas: Pam Meredith, principal; Lindsey Ray, second-grade teacher; and Kami Hinkle, first-grade teacher. At Brown Elementary in Irving, Texas: Adam Grinage, principal; Jennifer Putman, Instructional Specialist; and Sandy Hawkins, Kindergarten teacher.

A special thank-you and acknowledgment to my husband, Jacob, for his support as I wrote this book and believing in me from beginning to end, and to my parents, who have always encouraged me to follow my dreams and have stood behind me, no matter what.

How to Use This Book

What is a Ten-Frame?

Ten-Frame

This is a ten-frame:

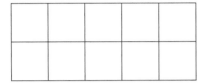

A ten-frame is a five-by-two array used to support the development of the important landmark numbers five and ten. In most of the lessons in this book, the ten-frame is positioned horizontally and filled with counters placed from left to right and top to bottom. In lessons designed to help students visualize numbers, counters are randomly placed on the ten-frame.

Double Ten-Frame

This is a double ten-frame:

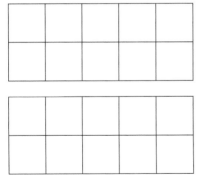

A double ten-frame is two ten-frames used to support the development of the important landmark numbers ten and twenty. It is also designed to support addition strategies (such as making a ten) and place-value ideas (such as building fourteen using one ten-frame filled with ten counters and a second ten-frame filled with four counters).

Ten-Frame Cards

These are ten-frame cards:

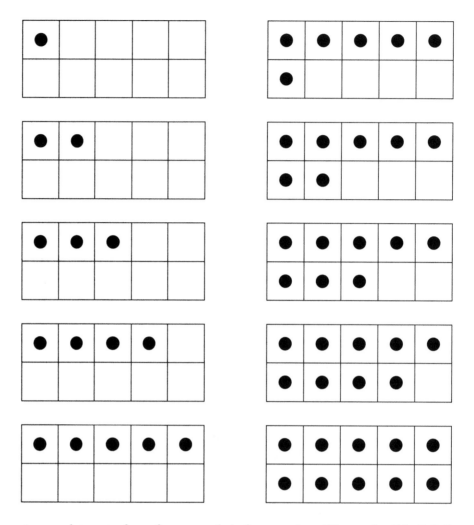

A complete set of ten-frame cards is four copies of Reproducible B. When the cards are cut apart, each deck should have forty cards ranging from one dot to ten dots. Ten-frame cards are used during lessons and activities to develop fluency with addition facts.

Why Use Ten-Frames?

State standards require students to solve addition and subtraction problems using a variety of strategies, including models. Ten-frames are a model to help students efficiently gain and develop an understanding of addition and subtraction. The lessons in this book use ten-frames to develop students' natural strategies for adding numbers. You'll find that the lessons fit into any set of state standards or curriculum. (See the "Chapter Connections to the NCTM Focal Points, K–2" table on page xxi for further guidance.)

Why These Lessons?

The lessons I selected for this book were tested in many classrooms across the United States, both through my work as a second-grade teacher and as an education specialist for Math Solutions. As a Math Solutions' education specialist, one of my favorite responsibilities is teaching student lessons while teachers observe. Many of the lessons have served as model lessons with kindergarten, first-, and second-grade students. Other lessons were ones that I used with my own classroom of second graders. I tried, revised, and tried again several lessons in Ms. Sandy Hawkins', Ms. Kami Hinkle's, and Ms. Lindsey Ray's kindergarten, first-, and second-grade classrooms.

I remember being unsure of how to use ten-frames when I was a new teacher. After attending professional development courses and learning the importance of providing opportunities for students to make sense of numbers, develop landmarks, and be able to compute flexibly and efficiently, I began to see the immense value and purpose of ten-frames in meeting those goals.

When I started working with Math Solutions, I encountered teachers who had the same initial hesitations I did about ten-frames. I found myself time and time again helping them become more comfortable and confident in using ten-frames based on my own successful experiences with the model. This led me to realize the need for a resource that provides teachers with rich lessons using ten-frames. I knew the ideas I was sharing with teachers needed to be widely accessible.

The classroom-tested lessons in *It Makes Sense! Using Ten-Frames to Build Number Sense* are first and foremost user-friendly. You can choose from a variety of lessons—each containing clear, concise directions—covering several number skills. The lessons are intentionally designed to provide students with opportunities to think, reason, and communicate about numbers. Many of the routines and games are intended to be revisited throughout the year to give students repeated experiences in building number sense.

How Do I Use the Lessons?

Using the Chapter Connections to the NCTM Focal Points, K–2 Table (page xxi)

The NCTM Focal Points focus on a number of key areas of emphasis for math teaching. Providing students with extended experiences in these core concepts and skills helps facilitate deep understanding, mathematical fluency, and the ability to generalize. The "Chapter Connections to the NCTM Focal Points, K–2" table gives an overview of the concepts and skills addressed in this book. Using the table alongside your own curriculum, standards, or pacing guides will help you determine which lessons meet the concepts and skills you're in need of addressing with your students.

Three Categories

The book is divided into three categories: routines, games, and problem-solving lessons. Each category opens with an introduction. Briefly, routines are short lessons that should be revisited several times a year in order to build students' sense of number. Games offer an engaging way for students to practice skills. Problem-solving lessons require extended time where students are asked to think and reason in order to deepen their understanding of number.

Where to Start

In the "Related Lessons" section of each lesson, you'll get suggestions for what to teach next. When you first use ten-frames, I suggest starting with the routines *Look Quick!* (R-1) and *Make the Number* (R-2). *Make Five* (G-5) or *Collect Ten* (G-6) are great starting places for games. When students are comfortable with ten-frames, then introduce the problem-solving lessons.

Lesson Overview

Each lesson opens with an overview that gives you an opportunity to become acquainted with the mathematical goals of the lesson, as well as what students will be doing.

Time

The "Time" section of each lesson gives a general prediction of the time it will take to carry out the lesson. Generally, each routine takes five to twenty minutes and is meant to be repeated throughout the school year; each game takes ten to thirty minutes; and each problem-solving lesson requires a full class period.

Materials

Following is a basic list of materials needed for the lessons; each lesson opens with a specific list. When possible, reproducibles are provided for your convenience.

▶ 1 ten-frame for each student (Reproducible A)

▶ 1 double ten-frame for each student (Reproducible D)

▶ 1 set of ten-frame cards for each pair of students. (Reminder: A set of ten-frame cards means four copies of Reproducible B, for a total of forty cards when cut apart.)

▶ 1 demonstration ten-frame (Reproducible A enlarged with document cameras or overheads; demonstration ten-frames can also easily be created on interactive whiteboards by inserting and enlarging a five-by-two-inch table.)

▶ 20 counters per student (For consistency, the term *counters* is used throughout this book. There are a variety of options for counters: Snap Cubes, Unifix cubes, color tiles, or two-color counters. You may also consider using everyday objects such as lima beans, pennies, dimes, or small buttons.)

Key Questions

Each lesson offers key questions to promote student thinking, class discussions, and the ability to assess what students know. These carefully planned questions elicit deeper thinking and reasoning among students and are meant to be asked throughout the lesson. Often it is necessary to scribe or record student thinking. Recording student thinking connects a child's thinking to representations, such as pictures, or symbols, such as numbers. It allows the student who is speaking and others in the class to visually observe their thinking.

Teaching Directions

The directions are presented in a step-by-step lesson plan with references to when and how to use the key questions and what a student might be thinking. Some of the lessons are divided into parts to make the planning process more manageable.

Additional Teaching Insights

In addition to the above, teaching insights are provided throughout the lessons in the following ways:

▶ "Math Matters!" sections provide an opportunity to deepen one's own math content;

▶ "Teaching Tip" and "Technology Tip" sections offer insights to help make the lesson run smoothly;

▶ "A Child's Mind . . ." sections give an opportunity to read how or why your own students may think about a problem;

▶ "Differentiating Your Instruction" sections offer extensions or modifications to meet all learners' needs;

▶ "Time Saver" sections provide insights for saving time in lesson preparation.

▶ "Extend Their Learning!" sections are featured in some lessons to continue the learning of groups of students or the whole class; and

▶ "Teacher Reflections" sections are included throughout the book to offer insight into experiences that have shaped my own thinking about teaching.

Chapter Connections to the NCTM Focal Points, K–2

NCTM Focal Point	Look, Quick! (R.1)	Make the Number (R.2)	Say the Two-Digit Number (R.3)	Number Strings (R.4)	Adding Nine (R.5)	Sums of More Than Ten (R.6)	Memory Games (G.1, G.2, and G.3)	More or Less (G.4)	Make Five (G.5)	Collect Ten (G.6)	Bank It! (G.7)	Double Bank It! (G.8)	Race to 20 (G.9)	Two-Color Counters (P.1)	Riddles (P.2)	Mystery Sums (P.3)	Adding and Subtracting Ten (P.4)	Partial Sums (P.5)
Kindergarten Number and Operation: Representing, comparing, and ordering whole numbers and joining and separating sets. Children use numbers, including written numerals, to represent quantities and to solve quantitative problems, such as counting objects in a set, creating a set with a given number of objects, comparing and ordering sets or numerals by using both cardinal and ordinal meanings, and modeling simple joining and separating situations with objects. They choose, combine, and apply effective strategies for answering quantitative questions, including quickly recognizing the number in a small set, counting and producing sets of given seizes, counting the number in combined sets and counting backward.	X	X	X				X	X	X	X	X		X					

(continued)

NCTM Focal Point	Look, Quick! (R.1)	Make the Number (R.2)	Say the Two-Digit Number (R.3)	Number Strings (R.4)	Adding Nine (R.5)	Sums of More Than Ten (R.6)	Memory Games (G.1, G.2, and G.3)	More or Less (G.4)	Make Five (G.5)	Collect Ten (G.6)	Bank It! (G.7)	Double Bank It! (G.8)	Race to 20 (G.9)	Two-Color Counters (P.1)	Riddles (P.2)	Mystery Sums (P.3)	Adding and Subtracting Ten (P.4)	Partial Sums (P.5)
First Grade Number and Operation and Algebra: Developing understanding of addition and subtraction and strategies for basic addition facts and related subtraction facts. Children develop strategies for adding and subtracting whole numbers on the basis of their earlier work with small numbers. They use a variety of models, including discrete objects, length bases models and number lines to model part–whole, adding to, taking away from, and comparing situations to develop an understanding of the meanings of addition and subtraction and strategies to solve such arithmetic problems. Children understand the connections between counting and the operations of addition and subtraction. They use properties of addition to add whole numbers, and they create and use increasingly sophisticated strategies based on these properties (e.g., making tens) to solve addition and subtraction problems involving basic facts. By comparing a variety of solution strategies, children relate addition and subtraction as inverse operations.	X	X			X	X		X	X	X	X	X		X	X	X	X	X

(continued)

NCTM Focal Point	Look, Quick! (R.1)	Make the Number (R.2)	Say the Two-Digit Number (R.3)	Number Strings (R.4)	Adding Nine (R.5)	Sums of More Than Ten (R.6)	Memory Games (G.1, G.2, and G.3)	More or Less (G.4)	Make Five (G.5)	Collect Ten (G.6)	Bank It! (G.7)	Double Bank It! (G.8)	Race to 20 (G.9)	Two-Color Counters (P.1)	Riddles (P.2)	Mystery Sums (P.3)	Adding and Subtracting Ten (P.4)	Partial Sums (P.5)
First Grade Number and Operations: Develop an understanding of whole number relationships, including grouping in tens and ones. Children compare and order whole numbers to develop an understanding of and solve problems involving the relative sizes of these numbers. They think of whole numbers between ten and one hundred in terms of groups of tens and ones. They understand the sequential order of counting numbers and their relative magnitudes and represent numbers on a number line.			X										X					

(continued)

NCTM Focal Point	Look, Quick! (R.1)	Make the Number (R.2)	Say the Two-Digit Number (R.3)	Number Strings (R.4)	Adding Nine (R.5)	Sums of More Than Ten (R.6)	Memory Games (G.1, G.2, and G.3)	More or Less (G.4)	Make Five (G.5)	Collect Ten (G.6)	Bank It! (G.7)	Double Bank It! (G.8)	Race to 20 (G.9)	Two-Color Counters (P.1)	Riddles (P.2)	Mystery Sums (P.3)	Adding and Subtracting Ten (P.4)	Partial Sums (P.5)
Second Grade Number and Operation: Developing an understanding of the base-ten numeration system and place-value concepts. Children develop an understanding of the base-ten numerations system and the place-value concepts. Their understanding of base-ten numeration includes ideas of counting in units and multiples of hundreds, tens, and ones, as well as a grasp of number relationships, which they demonstrate in a variety of ways, including comparing and ordering numbers. They understand multidigit numbers in terms of place value, recognizing that place-value notation is a shorthand for the sums of multiples of powers of 10.										X	X							X

(continued)

NCTM Focal Point	Look, Quick! (R.1)	Make the Number (R.2)	Say the Two-Digit Number (R.3)	Number Strings (R.4)	Adding Nine (R.5)	Sums of More Than Ten (R.6)	Memory Games (G.1, G.2, and G.3)	More or Less (G.4)	Make Five (G.5)	Collect Ten (G.6)	Bank It! (G.7)	Double Bank It! (G.8)	Race to 20 (G.9)	Two-Color Counters (P.1)	Riddles (P.2)	Mystery Sums (P.3)	Adding and Subtracting Ten (P.4)	Partial Sums (P.5)
Second Grade Number and Operations and Algebra: Developing quick recall of addition facts and related subtraction facts and fluency with multidigit addition and subtraction.																		
Children use their understanding of addition to develop quick recall of basic addition fats and related subtraction facts. They solve arithmetic problems by applying their understanding of models of addition and subtraction, relationships and properties of number, and properties of addition. Children develop, discuss, and use efficient, accurate, and generalizable methods to add and subtract multidigit whole numbers. They select and apply appropriate methods to estimate sums and differences or calculate them mentally, depending on the context and numbers involved. They develop fluency with efficient procedures, including standard algorithms, for adding and subtracting whole numbers, understand why the procedures work, and use them to solve problems.			X		X	X		X	X	X	X	X	X		X	X	X	

It Makes Sense!

Using Ten-Frames to Build Number Sense

Grades K–2

Routines Using Ten-Frames

What is a routine?

Routines are short (five- to twenty-minute), intentional minilessons that develop or foster new learning about number. Mathematical routines give teachers an opportunity to revisit skills from the previous year or unit and give students the opportunity to practice skills in an environment that values communication and problem solving. Teachers often feel pressured by pacing guides, testing dates, and the need to move on to other content. Routines allow teachers to spend a small amount of time on skills that develop students' number sense and basic computation without disrupting the flow of their structured curriculum.

Why these routines?

I chose the routines featured in this section because they are outstanding at helping students develop a sense of number and the ability to compute efficiently. I've used these routines in many classrooms; time and time again they prove to me that students benefit greatly from repeated experiences with talking about and making sense of quantities, part-whole relationships, and strategies for learning basic facts. Because these routines are revisited throughout the year, they engage students in the gradual process needed to help students understand number and build basic fact fluency. They are, simply put, timeless.

When should I teach with routines?

Traditionally routines are presented every day, at the beginning of the math class. However, you can use routines to start the day, end the day, or compensate for extra time throughout the day. Some teachers use routines during the fifteen minutes before or after lunch. It is helpful to set a time for routines and stick to that time. When routine times are set, teachers can begin to promote independence by letting students know at what time the routine will begin every day. If students will need counters, Snap Cubes, ten-frames, or other materials to complete the routine, consider writing that as a message on the board so students know that as soon as routine time is about to begin, they should go get the required materials. An alternative to this practice, described in several of the routines, involves students in assembling materials at the beginning of the day or math time so the materials are ready for you to distribute at the appropriate time.

How do I decide on a routine?

Let your students drive the routines you focus on. Observing students during a lesson can give valuable information and can provide the knowledge you need to select a routine. If you notice students are struggling with their addition facts for nine, spend time working on the *Adding Nine* routine. If you notice students are struggling to recognize numbers when they roll a standard die, spend time on the *Look, Quick!* routine.

Use certain routines over time—not every day—until students demonstrate mastery. It is not necessary, for example, to present the *Look, Quick!* routine every day until every child is subitizing numbers. It is more beneficial to present *Look, Quick!* once or twice a week for an extended period of time.

Routine 1

Look, Quick!

Math Matters!

Subitizing

The ability to glance at a group of objects and quickly see how many there are without counting them one by one. (See *Math Matters: Understanding the Math You Teach, Grades K–8, Second Edition* by Suzanne H. Chapin and Art Johnson, © 2006 Math Solutions.)

Time

5–10 minutes; repeat several times during the year

Materials

demonstration ten-frame (see Reproducible A)

counters, 10

Overview

In this routine, the teacher shows students counters on a ten-frame and asks them to look for groupings they see without counting. The ability to see groups of objects is known as *subitizing*. Subitizing helps students count quickly and learn to count on. The routine develops students' ability to see and recognize groups of numbers instead of always counting from one to the last object. Students also link the groupings they see to number sentences.

Related Lesson

Consider this lesson as a follow-up:

▶ R-2 Make the Number

Key Questions

▶ How many counters do you see?

▶ How did you know how many counters were on the ten-frame?

▶ How do you see the counters on the ten-frame?

Teaching Directions

1. Show students a blank demonstration ten-frame and ask them, "How many squares are there?" Turn it 90 degrees and ask the question again.

Example 1: Using Five Counters

2. Tell students that you are going to place some counters in the squares on the ten-frame. Students will need to determine the total number of counters you've placed. Ask students to close their eyes (alternatively, you can put the ten-frame out of sight while you place the counters). Place five counters in various squares on the demonstration ten-frame.

Five-counter example

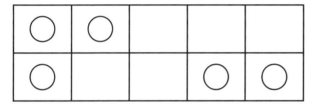

3. Reveal the ten-frame and ask students, "How many counters do you see?" Ask students to whisper, on the count of three, the total number of counters they see.

4. After students have whispered the number of counters, ask them, "How did you know how many counters were on the ten-frame?" Model a think-aloud to demonstrate how to look for groupings of counters.

5. Ask students if there is another way (besides the think-aloud you modeled) to see how the counters are grouped. Ask, "How do *you* see the counters on the ten-frame?"

Example 2: Using Four Counters

6. Repeat the activity, this time placing four counters on the demonstration ten-frame. Make sure students don't see you placing the counters!

A Child's Mind . . .

While it is obvious to adults that the number of squares stays the same regardless of how the ten-frame is positioned, it may not be to young students. Primary-aged students are still developing conservation of number.

Math Matters!

Conservation of Number
The understanding that the number of objects remains the same when they are rearranged spatially. (See *Math Matters: Understanding the Math You Teach, Grades K–8, Second Edition* by Suzanne H. Chapin and Art Johnson, © 2006 Math Solutions.)

Teaching Tip

Modeling a Think-Aloud
When encouraging students to think about groupings, model a think-aloud. For instance, for the five-counter example shown here, say, "Two counters are grouped together on the bottom right row and three are grouped together on the left side." Record 2 + 3 = 5 to help students connect your thinking to the symbolic notation.

A Child's Mind . . .

It is important to not show favoritism for one student's method for determining the total. The student who says he saw the counters as 1 + 1 + 1 + 1 + 1 = 5 will not feel validated if the student who sees it as 3 + 2 = 5 receives all the praise.

Teaching Tip

The Equal Sign

Many students only see equations written like 2 + 4 = 6 or 10 – 5 = 5. Constantly seeing and writing equations in this format leads students to develop an incorrect notion that the equal sign means the answer is coming. Change it up; try writing 6 = 4 + 2 or 5 = 10 – 5. This helps students understand that the equal sign means both sides should balance, or have the same value. It will also benefit students in later years when they begin to study more formalized algebraic concepts.

Teaching Tip

Emphasize Quickness!

In a classroom of students, there are several ideas of how to determine the amount of counters on the ten-frame. Some students may still be counting by ones while others are using grouping strategies. When you repeat this routine, begin by emphasizing that the goal is to look for *quick* ways to determine how many counters are on the ten-frame. A quick way to do so is by looking for *groups* of counters. **Note:** The ability to see groups of counters and use those groupings to determine the amount of counters on the ten-frame develops with repeated experiences.

Four-counter example A

	○	○	○	
				○

7. Show the ten-frame to the class and ask students to determine how many counters you have placed on it. "How many counters do you see?" Encourage them to look for groupings of counters. Ask students to whisper, on the count of three, the total number of counters they see.

8. Ask a volunteer to explain how he knew how many counters were on the ten-frame.

9. Introduce another mathematically correct method for writing a number sentence. Record *4*, then write an equal sign. Then record the volunteer student's explanation. For example, *4 = 2 + 2* or *4 = 1 + 1 + 1 + 1.*

10. After students are comfortable with looking for groups of numbers to find the total number of counters on the ten-frame, introduce the *Look, Quick!* routine. Explain to students that this time you will show them the ten-frame with counters on it, but they will have only three seconds to look at it. In this short amount of time, students need to figure out how many counters are on the ten-frame. Remind them to look for groups of numbers they see rather than count the individual counters.

11. Repeat the activity, once again placing four counters on the ten-frame, but in different groupings than before. Make sure students aren't looking!

Four-counter example B

◯				◯
◯				◯

12. Reveal the ten-frame for three seconds, then cover it up. "How many counters did you see?" Ask students to whisper, on the count of three, the total number of counters they saw.

13. Ask students, "How did you know how many counters were on the ten-frame?" or "How did you see the counters?" When a student shares her idea, record the corresponding number sentence, starting with the sum first. For example: 4 = 2 + 2.

Example 3: Using Six Counters

14. Repeat the routine, this time placing six counters on the ten-frame.

Six-counter example

◯	◯	◯		◯
◯				◯

15. Reveal the ten-frame for three seconds, then cover it up. "How many counters did you see?" Ask students to whisper, on the count of three, the total number of counters they saw.

16. Ask students, "How did you know how many counters were on the ten-frame?" or "How did you see the counters?" When a student shares his idea, record the corresponding number sentence, starting with the sum first.

17. Repeat this activity several times. Consider using the same number of counters but repositioning them each time on the ten-frame.

Differentiating Your Instruction

Positioning Counters
Choose a certain number of counters and reposition them each time on the demonstration ten-frame so students will be successful. As time goes on, use more counters or position them in more challenging ways.

Teacher Reflection

My *Look, Quick!* Experiences

Intervention

The first time I learned about the *Look, Quick!* routine, I questioned why it was important and how it would help students. The answer didn't come to me for many years; when it did, it truly affected my understanding of why opportunities to foster subitizing are crucial with young learners.

The moment happened when I was working with second graders who were identified as intervention students—students who were struggling in the regular classroom. The multiplication unit was coming up and it was decided to front-load the students with intervention lessons on multiplication. We started by playing a well-known game called *Circles and Stars*. During this game, a player rolls a die and then draws the corresponding number of circles on a piece of paper. Then the player rolls the die again and draws the corresponding number of stars in each circle. I watched as Pedro drew four circles and three stars in each circle. When I asked him how many stars he saw, he proceeded to count the first set of stars by ones. "One, two three," he said timidly. He then continued counting the stars, one by one, until he reached twelve.

I wanted to see if Pedro could subitize, so I asked, "Pedro, how many stars are in the first circle?" He looked blankly at me, then at the first circle, and once again began to count by ones.

I clarified, "Pedro, can you tell how many stars there are by just looking quickly at the circle?" I drew another circle with two stars and asked him how many stars he saw.

Again, he looked at me, then, studying the circle, carefully counted, "One, two." I wondered if Pedro had had opportunities in kindergarten, first grade, or second grade to subitize numbers through activities such as *Look, Quick!* It became clear to me that his struggle to see groups of numbers was impeding his development of addition and multiplication. How could he start to think multiplicatively if he didn't see numbers as groups? How could he begin to count on when adding if he still needed to begin at one?

Make the Number

Overview

In this routine, the teacher quickly shows students a ten-frame with counters. Using their own ten-frames and counters, students then build what they just saw in the same configuration. The routine combines the ability to subitize with spatial reasoning.

Related Lessons

You might teach the following lessons first:

▶ R-1 Look, Quick!

▶ G-5 Make Five

Consider this lesson as a follow-up:

▶ G-2 Numeral Memory

Key Questions

▶ How many counters did you use?

▶ What did you build first?

▶ How did you know where to place the counters?

▶ What did you see?

▶ How did you see it?

Time

5–15 minutes; repeat several times during the year

Materials

demonstration ten-frame (see Reproducible A)

ten-frames (Reproducible A), 1 per student

counters, 10 for the teacher and 10 per student

Extension

ten-frames (Reproducible A), 1 per student

counters, 10 per student

sheets of construction paper or file folders, 1 per pair of students

Time Saver

As students are settling in for the day, ask the first two students who arrive to help with preparing the day's math materials. These students can count out groups of ten counters and place each group in a plastic sandwich bag. This makes it easy to distribute the counters when it comes time to do so. Alternatively, have each student count out a group of ten counters as soon as he or she enters the room. Once again, students can place their counters in plastic sandwich bags so you can easily distribute the materials when the time comes to do so.

Teaching Tip

Partner Talk

Have each student turn and talk to a classmate seated near him or her. Use this time to circulate, listening in on conversations and making note of key comments and concerns.

A Child's Mind . . .

Showing the demonstration ten-frame for only three seconds might seem like hardly any time at all, but keep in mind that this routine is focused on helping students subitize (glance at a group of objects and quickly see how many there are without counting them one by one). Often when I observe students during this routine, I notice that many are able to use the correct number of counters, but placing them in the same position on their ten-frames is more difficult. Over time, students are able to better visualize the ten-frame and counters and are more successful placing the counters in the correct spot.

Teaching Directions

1. Give each student a ten-frame and ten counters. Ask students to keep their counters off the ten-frames until the routine begins.

2. Begin with an example. Place three counters on a demonstration ten-frame. Leave the ten-frame in sight. Instruct students, "Build what you see." When they are ready, ask students to whisper how many counters they used. Finally, have students turn and talk to their partners about what they built.

3. Ask students to clear their ten-frames.

4. Explain to students, "This time, I will show the ten-frame for only three seconds." Again, place three counters on the ten-frame, but in a different arrangement than before. Show the demonstration ten-frame for three seconds. Ask students to build, on their ten-frames, what they remember seeing.

5. When students are finished building, ask the class these key questions:

    ▶ How many counters did you use?

    ▶ What did you build first?

    ▶ How did you know where to place the counters?

    Give students time to talk to their partners about these questions before starting a whole-class discussion.

6. Show the demonstration ten-frame again and give students time to check what they built and correct any mistakes.

7. Repeat this routine a few more times. Ideally, revisit it several times a month.

Differentiating Your Instruction

Positioning Counters

Start by grouping counters together or at the ends of the demonstration ten-frame. When it is time to challenge the class, spread the counters out more (leaving squares between them).

Extend Their Learning!

Give students the opportunity to do this routine on their own, in pairs. Provide each pair with two ten-frames, twenty counters, and a sheet of construction paper or a file folder.

First model a few rounds with a volunteer partner. Explain to students that each set of partners has two jobs: the builder job and the maker job. Each person must have the opportunity to do both jobs. The builder is in charge of placing some counters on her ten-frame. The maker is not allowed to look as the builder does this (preferably the maker closes and covers his eyes with his hands). When the builder says, "Go!" she reveals the ten-frame and counts slowly to three as the maker studies the ten-frame. The builder then covers the ten-frame with a piece of construction paper or file folder. It's now the maker's turn to build what he just saw, using his own ten-frame. Partners then compare the two ten-frames. It's the builder's job to ask the following key questions:

What did you see?

How did you see it?

For each new round, partners should switch jobs.

Teaching Tip

Wait Time

Model how—and the pace at which—the builder should count to three. It may be helpful to ask builders to count by hundreds, for example, "One hundred, two hundred, three hundred." Also model correct and incorrect ways for the maker to wait until the builder reveals the ten-frame. Discuss which way is correct and why.

Teaching Tip

Asking Questions

Post the key questions in the classroom so all students have access to them. Alternatively, print out copies of the questions for each pair to refer to.

Teaching Tip

Number of Counters

Consider first giving one ten-frame and five counters to each student. As you circulate and observe partners, note those who have mastered this extension; allow them to work with more than five counters.

Teacher Reflection

My *Make the Number* Experiences
Accommodating All Learners

I recently helped implement the extension of this routine in Sandy Hawkin's kindergarten class. After a student volunteer and I modeled several rounds for everyone, students eagerly began playing in pairs. As I walked around, I was pleased to see how seriously the students were taking on their jobs. The makers were carefully keeping their eyes covered while the builders arranged their sets of five counters on the ten-frames. In turn, the builders were remembering to ask the makers the key questions (which were posted in the front of the room). I made it a point to watch each pair for one complete round before moving to the next. I noted a variety of comfort levels, ranging from students who were quickly ready to work with more than five counters to students who were unable to subitize the number of counters and re-create the correct placement.

For students who were struggling, I asked the builders to work with three counters. This might have felt disruptive to some students, but these students were accustomed to having me modify the activities as they were engaged with them. When working with kindergartners, I always relate such actions to reading; I explain to the children that just as we change the books we read

FIGURE R-2.1 During the extension, Kylie covers her eyes as Mireya places counters on her ten frame.

FIGURE R-2.2 Mireya checks Kylie's work and confirms that she created what Mireya had originally built.

in our reading groups, we can also change the tools we use in math—for example, using three counters instead of five.

On subsequent days, I had the students do the routine again or alternatively play the game *Make Five* (see G-5 in the "Games" section of this book). While this was happening, I worked with small groups of students who were struggling with *Make the Number*.

Routine 3   Say the Two-Digit Number

Time

20 minutes

Materials

demonstration ten-frame cards (see Reproducible B), 1 set

demonstration ten-frame card with ten dots (see Reproducible C), 5

Extension

demonstration ten-frame cards (see Reproducible B), 1 set

demonstration ten-frame card with ten dots (see Reproducible C), 5

ten-frame cards (Reproducible B), 1 set per pair of students

extras of the ten-frame card with ten dots (Reproducible C), 5 per pair of students

Overview

In this routine, the teacher quickly shows students a two-digit number represented via ten-frame cards and then asks them to figure out the number (by determining the total number of dots displayed). The teacher pays special attention to how students figure out the number. The routine develops students' ability to see two-digit numbers as tens and ones (or leftovers). Use of the ten-frame cards provides an opportunity to introduce formal place-value vocabulary. To extend the learning, the teacher gives students an opportunity to work in pairs to build the two-digit number using their own sets of ten-frame cards. Throughout the routine, the class makes connections to the place value and expanded notation of the numbers.

Related Lessons

You might teach the following lesson first:

▶ R-1 Look Quick!

Consider these lessons as a follow-up:

▶ G-9 Race to 20
▶ P-5 Partial Sums

Key Questions

▶ How many dots did you see?
▶ How did you see them?

Teaching Directions

1. Explain to students that you are going to place some ten-frame cards on display in front of the class. They will need to figure out the total number of dots they see. Ask them to look for *groups* of dots to help their calculations. Let them know that they will get to see the cards for only three seconds.

Example 1: One Card with Ten Dots and One Card with Five Dots

2. Display a ten-frame card with ten dots and a ten-frame card with five dots. Give students just three seconds to look at the two cards.

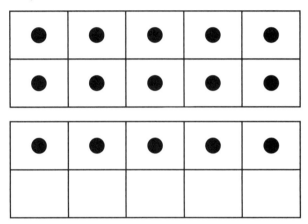

3. Place the cards out of sight and ask students to whisper the total number of dots they saw.

4. Display the same two cards again. Ask students to turn to their partners and talk about how they knew the total. Refer students to the key questions to help their discussions.

5. Call on students to explain their thinking. Record their explanations to help them connect their thinking to the symbolic notation.

> **Examples of Student Thinking**
>
> "I saw ten and counted on five more." (Record *10, 11, 12, 13, 14, 15.*)
>
> "I saw ten and five, and that's fifteen." (Record *10 + 5 = 15.*)

Technology Tip

Displaying Ten-Frame Cards on an Interactive Whiteboard
Consider using an interactive whiteboard to display the ten-frame cards. Use the shade to cover up the cards. Then lower the shade to show the cards and raise the shade to cover them again.

Example 2: Two Cards with Ten Dots and One Card with Three Dots

6. Tell students that you are now going to put a different set of cards on display. They will get three seconds to look at the cards. Encourage them to look for groups of dots.

7. Display two ten-frame cards with ten dots each and one ten-frame card with three dots. Display the cards so that the card with three dots is in the middle. Give students only three seconds to look at the cards.

8. Place the cards out of sight and ask students to whisper the total number of dots they saw.

9. Display the same three cards again. Ask students to turn to their partners and talk about how they knew the total. Refer students to the key questions to help their discussions.

10. Call on students to explain their thinking. Record their explanations to help them connect their thinking to the symbolic notation.

ⓘ Teaching Tip ———

Asking Questions
Post the key questions in the classroom so all students have access to them.

Examples of Student Thinking

"I counted ten, twenty, and three more."
(Record *10, 20, 21, 22, 23.*)

"I saw ten and ten and three and knew that was twenty-three."
(Record *10 + 10 + 3 = 23.*)

"I saw ten and three and knew that was thirteen and counted on ten more since I saw another filled ten-frame card."
(Record *10 + 3 = 13; 14, 15, 16, 17, 18, 19, 20, 21, 22, 23.*)

11. Ask students if they found it easier to look for the groups of ten first and then count on or add on the other groups of dots. Have a few students discuss with the class why a certain process was easier for them. Encourage the whole class to look for groups of ten first and then count or add the remaining dots.

Example 3: Two Cards with Ten Dots and One Card with Seven Dots

12. Display two ten-frame cards with ten dots and one ten-frame card with seven dots. Display the cards so that the card with seven dots is in the middle. Give students three seconds to look at the cards.

13. Place the cards out of sight and ask students to whisper the total number of dots they saw.

14. Display the same three cards again. Ask students to turn to their partners and talk about how they knew the total. Once again, refer students to the key questions to help their discussions.

15. Call on students to explain their thinking. Record their explanations to help students connect their thinking to the symbolic notation.

16. Refer to what you've recorded. Underline the 7 in the total number of dots, 27. Ask the class where the 7 is represented in the cards. Next underline the 2 in the 27 and ask the class where the 2 is represented in the cards.

17. Discuss the meaning of the digits and their connections to the cards. Introduce the terms *place value*, *tens place*, and *ones place* as you make connections to students' answers.

18. Look for opportunities to connect what students are saying to ways to record *27 = 20 + 7* and *27 = 2 tens and 3 ones.*

Example 4: Four Cards with Ten Dots and One Card with Three Dots

19. Display four ten-frame cards with ten dots and one ten-frame card with three dots. Display the cards so that the card with three dots is in the beginning or middle. Give students three seconds to look at the cards.

Teaching Tip

Supporting ELLs
It's helpful for students, especially English language learners, if you display new words somewhere that they can see them. Record the words *tens place* and *ones place* on the word wall in your classroom. Alternatively, display a number and under the corresponding places, write the words *tens place* and *ones place*. (See *Supporting English Language Learners in Math Class, Grades K–2* by Rusty Bresser, Kathy Melanese, and Christine Sphar, © 2009 Math Solutions.)

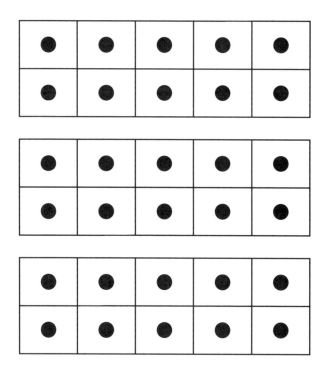

20. Place the cards out of sight and ask students to whisper the total number of dots they saw.

21. Display the same five cards again. Ask students to turn to their partners and talk about how they knew the total. Once again, refer students to the key questions to help their discussions.

22. Call on students to explain their thinking. Record their explanations to help students connect their thinking to the symbolic notation.

23. Refer to what you've recorded. Underline the 3 in the total number of dots, 43. Ask the class where 3 is represented in the cards. Next underline the 4 in the 43 and ask the class where the 4 is represented in the cards. As students discuss, look for opportunities to record both *43 = 40 + 3* and *43 = 4 tens and 3 ones.*

24. Repeat this routine a few times a month as needed to help students develop their understanding of place value.

Extend Their Learning!

Give students the opportunity, in pairs, to build the numbers they see. First give a set of ten-frame cards and five extras of the ten-frame card marked with ten dots to each pair of students (the extra cards will allow students to build any two-digit number). Explain to students that you are going to place some ten-frame cards on display in front of the class. With their partners, students will need to use their own ten-frame cards to build what they see. Let them know that they will get to see the cards for only three to five seconds.

FIGURE R-3.1 Mrs. Ray's class figures out how many dots they see.

FIGURE R-3.2 When students are ready they begin to raise their hands.

Display three ten-frame cards with ten dots and one ten-frame card with two dots. Display the cards in any order. Give students just three to five seconds to look at the cards. Place the cards out of sight and ask students to work together to build what they saw.

Ask students to whisper the total number of dots they saw. Record *32* on the board and ask, "How many ten-frame cards with ten dots did I use?" Then ask, "What card was left over?" Remind students that mathematicians call the leftovers the *ones place*. Next to 32, record = *3 tens and 2 ones*. Ask students, "How can three tens and two ones be written as a number sentence?" Give them time to talk to their partners before calling on a volunteer. Record the number sentence, preferably *32 = 30 + 2*.

Tell students to clear their space and get ready to see the next number. This time display six ten-frame cards with ten dots and one ten-frame card with one dot. Display the cards in any order. Give students three to five seconds to look at the cards. Place the cards out of sight and ask students to work together to build what they saw.

FIGURE R-3.3 Lionel explains how he knew how many dots he saw.

Ask students to whisper the total number of dots they saw. Record *61* on the board and ask, "How many ten-frame cards with ten dots did I use?" Then ask, "What card was left over?" Next to 61, record *= 6 tens and 1 one*. Ask students to turn to their partners and discuss what number sentence would match the words *6 tens and 1 one*. Call on a volunteer. Record the number sentence, preferably *61 = 60 + 1*.

Routine 4

Number Strings

Time

Part 1: 10–20 minutes

Part 2: 10–20 minutes

Part 3: 20 minutes

Repeat each part several times during the year.

Materials

demonstration ten-frame cards (see Reproducible B), 1 set

ten-frame cards (Reproducible B), 1 set per pair of students

demonstration double ten-frame (see Reproducible D)

double ten-frame (Reproducible D), 1 per student or pair of students

Snap Cubes or counters, 20 for the teacher and 20 per student

Extension

Number Strings recording sheet (Reproducible 1), 1 copy per student

double ten-frame (Reproducible D), 1 per student

counters, 20 per student

Overview

In this two-part routine, the teacher shows students strings of three numbers using ten-frame cards and asks them to look for efficient ways to add the numbers. Number strings give students opportunities to think about using ten as a landmark for adding numbers as well as making and using doubles as an efficient addition strategy. Students gain a deeper experience by looking at the entire string to find numbers they can efficiently add instead of adding from left to right by rote. Whole-class discussions provide a forum for building number strings, explaining addition strategies, and discussing solution strategies.

Related Lessons

You might teach the following lessons first:

▶ R-5 Adding Nine

▶ G-6 Collect Ten

Key Questions

▶ Which two numbers would you like to add first?

▶ Which numbers are friendly to add? Why?

▶ How can making a ten help you solve the problem?

▶ How does knowing nine plus one help you solve nine plus two, and so on?

Teaching Directions

Part 1

1. Explain to students that you are going to display three ten-frame cards. As a class, they must work together to find the sum. Tell students that they should look for two friendly numbers to add together first. Explain to students what you mean when you say "friendly numbers."

Example 1: 4 + 3 + 6

2. Display three ten-frame cards: one with four dots, one with three dots, and one with six dots. Ask students to say each number as you turn over the corresponding card. Record the matching number sentence: 4 + 3 + 6. This is the number string.

3. Ask students to look for two friendly numbers in the number string. These are the two numbers they should add together first. Record students' thinking. For example, students may choose the following combinations:

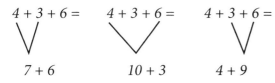

4. Now ask students to look at the number sentences you recorded and discuss which one has the friendliest two numbers to add. Typically students who have had experiences with ten-frames will say 10 + 3 is the easiest (friendliest) for them to add. When they do, record = 13 next to 10 + 3.

✚ Math Matters!

Friendly Numbers

Numbers that a student finds easy to work with and can add together quickly. Friendly numbers may be two numbers a student already knows the sum of because she has learned that fact. They also may be two numbers she can quickly add because she can use a strategy such as counting on or making a ten. (See *Math Matters: Understanding the Math You Teach, Grades K–8, Second Edition* by Suzanne H. Chapin and Art Johnson, © 2006 Math Solutions.)

ⓘ Teaching Tip

Pocket Charts

Using a pocket chart to hold the three demonstration ten-frame cards as you reveal them is especially helpful in this routine.

Teaching Tip

Choosing Numbers

The numbers you choose play an important role in number strings. In this example, I choose to start with four, three, and six because my students have already played *Collect Ten* (see G-6 in the "Games" section of this book) several times and I want them to look for combinations of ten. My students typically have also experienced the routine *Adding Nine* (see R-5) and discussed strategies for adding nine during previous minilessons. If students choose to add six and three first, this then gives them an opportunity to practice adding nine.

5. Ask students to look at the number sentence 4 + 9. Using a demonstration double ten-frame, build the number sentence with counters.

6. Ask students, "How many counters can be moved from the ten-frame with four counters to make the ten-frame with nine counters have ten counters?" Using the demonstration double ten-frame, model how moving one counter from the ten-frame with four counters to the ten-frame with nine makes ten counters. Under the original 4 + 9 number sentence, record *4 + 9 = 3 + 10*. Ask students to check to see how much 10 + 3 is before recording *= 13* next to the original 4 + 9.

7. Now ask students to look at the number sentence 7 + 6. Build it on the demonstration double ten-frame.

8. Record 6 + 6 under the 7 + 6 and tell students that the double will help them solve the problem. Ask them what makes the first problem, 7 + 6, different from the second problem, 6 + 6. When they say seven is one more than six, tell them you are going to record 7 as *1 + 6*. Record *7 + 6 = 1 + 6 + 6*. Have students figure out what 6 + 6 is and then add 1 more. Record the sum next to the number sentence.

9. Ask students to look again at 7 + 6 on the demonstration double ten-frame and think about how making a ten could help them solve the problem. Model moving three counters from the six to make the seven a ten.

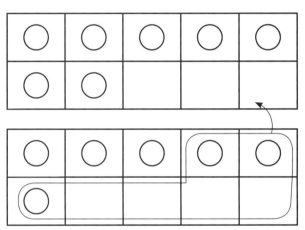

Record *7 + 6 = 10 + 3*.

10. Finally, record *= 13* next to the original 7 + 6 number sentence. Your recording space may look like the following:

$$4 + 3 + 6 = \qquad 4 + 3 + 6 = \qquad 4 + 3 + 6 =$$

$$7 + 6 = 13 \qquad 10 + 3 = 13 \qquad 4 + 9 = 13$$

$$6 + 6 = \qquad\qquad\qquad 4 + 9 =$$

$$10 + 3$$

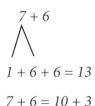

$$7 + 6$$

$$1 + 6 + 6 = 13$$

$$7 + 6 = 10 + 3$$

A Child's Mind . . .

As students continually reflect on number sentences that are friendliest for them, they begin to look at strings of numbers with an eye of choosing the most efficient way to add, rather than rotely adding left to right.

11. Bring students' attention back to the original number sentences and again ask them which was most friendly for them to add: 7 + 6, 10 + 3, or 4 + 9. As mentioned in Step 4 many students think adding 10 + 3 is easiest. Tell them they might want to look for a ten in the next number string that you display.

Example 2: 8 + 4 + 2

12. Display three new ten-frame cards: one with eight dots, one with four dots, and one with two dots. Ask students to say each number as you turn over the corresponding card. Record the matching number sentence: *8 + 4 + 2.*

13. Ask students to look for two friendly numbers in the number string and add those together first. Record students' thinking. For example, students may choose the following combinations:

$8 + 4 + 2 =$	$8 + 4 + 2 =$	$8 + 4 + 2 =$
$10 + 4$	$12 + 2$	$8 + 6$

14. Now ask students to look at the number sentences you recorded and discuss which one has the friendliest two numbers to add. Typically students will say 10 + 4 or 12 + 2 is the easiest (friendliest) for them to add. When they do, ask them to quietly figure out the sum.

15. Ask students to whisper the sum. Record the sum for the corresponding number sentences.

16. Now focus students' attention on the number sentence 8 + 6. Build it on the demonstration double ten-frame.

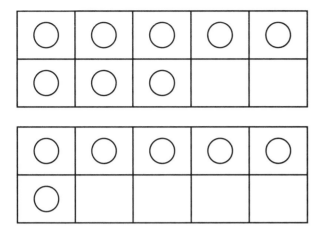

Ask students, "How can making a ten help us solve this problem?"

17. After students have had time to think and talk about your question, use the demonstration double ten-frame to model moving two from the six to complete a frame of ten.

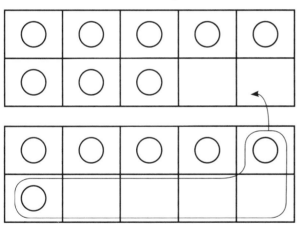

Record *8 + 6 = 10 + 4.*

Part 2

1. Give each student or pair of students twenty Snap Cubes or counters and one double ten-frame. Remind students of the previous number strings lesson (Part 1 of this routine). Explain to them that they will work to solve number strings again, but this time they will be able to use their own double

 Time Saver

As students are settling in for the day, ask the first two students who arrive to help with preparing the day's math materials. These students can count out groups of twenty counters and place each group in a plastic sandwich bag. This makes it easy to distribute the counters when it comes time to do so. Alternatively, have each student count out a group of twenty counters as soon as he or she enters the room. Once again, students can place their counters in plastic sandwich bags so you can easily distribute the materials when the time comes to do so.

ten-frames and counters. Make sure they know that you will tell them when it is time to begin using their double ten-frames.

Example 1: 5 + 2 + 7

2. Display three ten-frame cards: one with five dots, one with two dots, and one with seven dots. Ask students to say each number as you turn over the corresponding card. Record the matching number sentence: *5 + 2 + 7*.

3. Ask students to look for two friendly numbers in the number string. Remind students what the term *friendly* means (the two numbers they find easiest to add first). Record students' thinking.

Examples of Student Thinking

Note: Most primary students will not choose 5 + 7, but if it comes up, record it. If the students do not suggest it, you can introduce it as a possibility for them to consider.

4. Now ask students to look at the number sentences you recorded and discuss which one has the friendliest two numbers to add. Typically students will say 12 + 2 is the easiest for them to add. When they do, ask them to quietly figure out the sum.

5. Ask students to whisper the sum. Record the sum for the corresponding number sentence.

6. Next explain to students that mathematicians call 7 + 7 a *doubles fact*. Ask them, "Do you know the sum of seven plus seven?" If most students have not learned their doubles, build 7 + 7 on a demonstration double ten-frame. Instruct students to also build 7 + 7 on their own double ten-frames (or the ones they are sharing with their partners).

7. Ask students, "How can making a ten help us add seven plus seven?" After students have directed you to move three from the seven to make a ten, record *7 + 7 = 10 + 4*. Encourage students to practice moving three from the seven to make a ten on their double ten-frames.

8. Finally, ask students to figure out the sum and record it next to the original 7 + 7.

9. Now focus students' attention on the number sentence 5 + 9. Build it on the demonstration double ten-frame.

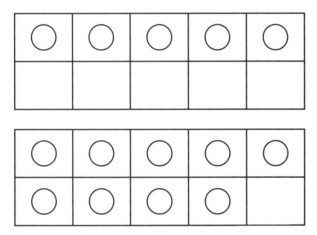

10. Instruct students to also build 5 + 9 on their own double ten-frames.

11. Ask students, "How can making a ten help us add five plus nine?" Give students time to build a ten on their double ten-frames.

12. Ask students to volunteer explaining how they made a ten. As students describe their thinking, model what they are saying.

Example of Student Thinking

"I moved one from the five to fill the frame with nine on it." (Record *5 + 9 = 4 + 10* under the original 5 + 9.)

13. Finally, ask students to figure out the sum and record it next to the original 5 + 9.

Example 2: 4 + 5 + 2

14. Display three new ten-frame cards: one with four dots, one with five dots, and one with

Teaching Tip

Using Snap Cubes
As an extension to Step 7, ask students to build two towers of seven using Snap Cubes. Then ask students to count the towers by twos to check the answer.

two dots. Ask students to say each number as you turn over the corresponding card. Record the matching number sentence: *4 + 5 + 2.*

15. Ask students to look for two friendly numbers in the number string. Remind students what the term *friendly* means. Record students' thinking.

Examples of Student Thinking

4 + 5 + 2	4 + 5 + 2	4 + 5 + 2
4 + 7	9 + 2	6 + 5

16. Now ask students to look at the number sentences you recorded and discuss which one has the friendliest two numbers to add. Students will likely choose 9 + 2 to add because it is close to 9 + 1. Discuss this with students; ask them if they know what 9 + 1 is and how that helps them think about 9 + 2.

17. Ask students to whisper the sum. Record the sum for the corresponding number sentence.

18. Now focus students' attention on the number sentence 4 + 7. Build it on the demonstration double ten-frame.

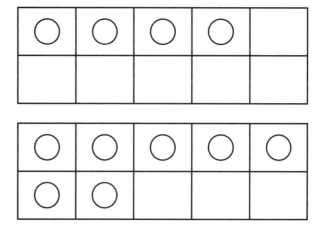

19. Instruct students to also build 4 + 7 on their own double ten-frames.

20. Ask students, "How can making a ten help us add four plus seven?" Give students time to think and discuss.

21. On the demonstration double ten-frame, model moving three from the four to fill the second frame.

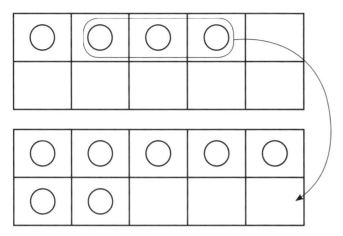

Record *4 + 7 = 1 + 10*. After students tell you what 1 + 10 is, record the sum next to the original 4 + 7 number sentence.

22. Focus students' attention on the number sentence 6 + 5. Build it on the demonstration double ten-frame.

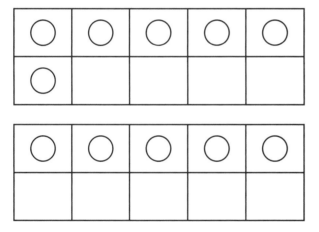

23. Instruct students to also build 6 + 5 on their own double ten-frames.

24. Ask students, "How can making ten help us to add six plus five?" Give students time to think and discuss.

25. On the demonstration double ten-frame, model moving four from the five to fill the first frame.

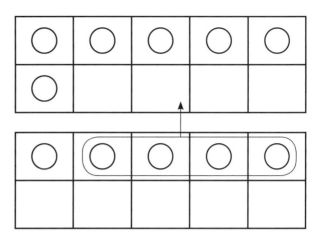

26. Record *6 + 5 = 10 + 1*. Record the sum next to the original 6 + 5 number sentence.

Example 3: Students Choose!

27. After you are confident with students' understanding of this routine, tell students that they will now have the opportunity to build their own number strings in pairs. Give each pair of students one set of ten-frame cards. Tell them to place the set in a stack, facedown. Instruct one student in each pair to draw three ten-frame cards from the top of the stack and say each number as he turns over the corresponding card. The other student must record the matching number sentence (the number string) and identify pairs of friendly numbers to add. Once partners have done so, ask them to add the third number to find the sum of the number string. Remind students to discuss their addition strategies with their partners. When they have finished with that number string, they set the three cards aside and the partners switch roles.

A Child's Mind . . .

Remind students that this is a routine, not a game, so there is no winner or loser. The purpose is to give students repeated experiences with adding number strings and discussing computation with other students.

Extend Their Learning!

Allow some groups of students to play one of the ten-frame games in this book while you work with small groups (four to five students) on the *Number Strings* recording sheet (Reproducible 1). Rotate the groups so each group has an opportunity to work on *the Number Strings* recording sheet with you.

Number Strings

Directions

Find the sums for the following number strings. You may use a set of ten-frame cards and/or a double ten-frame and counters to help you.

1. 2 + 6 + 4   6. 1 + 6 + 9

2. 5 + 3 + 8   7. 5 + 8 + 5

3. 8 + 4 + 2   8. 7 + 2 + 6

4. 7 + 5 + 3   9. 9 + 3 + 7

5. 5 + 4 + 1   10. 8 + 9 + 1

FIGURE R4-1 Reproducible 1: *Number Strings* recording sheet

Routine 5

Adding Nine

Time

20 minutes

Materials

store advertisements that list prices for items, a small assortment

demonstration double ten-frame (see Reproducible D)

double ten-frame (Reproducible D), 1 per pair of students

Adding Nine recording sheet (Reproducible 2), 1 copy per student

Snap Cubes or counters in two colors, 20 (ten of each color) for the teacher and 20 (ten of each color) per student

Extension 1

ten-frame cards (Reproducible B), 1 set per pair of students

double ten-frame (Reproducible D), 1 per pair of students

Extension 2

students' completed *Adding Nine* recording sheets (Reproducible 2)

Overview

In this routine, students use number relationships to look for patterns and connections between addends and sums when adding nine to other numbers. Students develop and apply the use of ten, a landmark number, to help them learn their addition facts for nine. The assessment asks students to find the sum of the nine facts so the teacher can see which nine facts the students can fluently add and which nine facts the teacher may want to focus on the next time the *Adding Nine* routine is taught.

Related Lessons

You might teach the following lessons first:

▶ G-5 Make Five

▶ G-6 Collect Ten

Consider these lessons as a follow-up:

▶ R-4 Number Strings

▶ R-6 Sums of More Than Ten

Key Questions

▶ How can making a ten help you solve this problem?

▶ What number sentence matches what we see?

▶ What do you notice about the number sentences?

Teaching Directions

1. Explain to students that the focus of this routine is developing strategies for adding nine to a number. Show students a store advertisement that lists prices for items. Ask them to notice all the prices that end in a 9. Discuss how stores often price things so they are $1.99 or $24.99; learning to add nine quickly is an important skill in life!

2. Write *9 + 6* on the board and acknowledge that this can be a tricky fact. Connect to students' prior learning by referring to *Collect Ten* (see G-6 in the "Games" section of this book), if appropriate, and telling them that the facts they know for adding ten will help them solve the facts for adding nine.

Example 1: 9 + 6

3. Using a demonstration double ten-frame, fill the first ten-frame with nine counters of one color and the second ten-frame with six counters of another color.

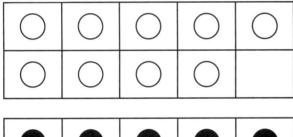

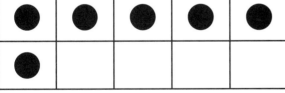

4. Tell students, "Using what we know about ten can help us solve nine plus six." Ask them, "What do we need to do to fill in the first ten-frame?" After students have answered, move the last counter from the second ten-frame to the top ten-frame.

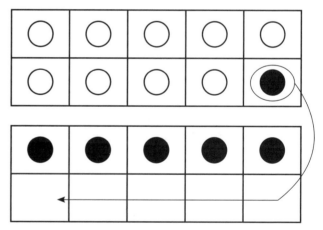

Differentiating Your Instruction

Think-pair-share allows all students time to process the question, think about an answer, and test out their thinking before having to speak in front of the whole class. This format also gives students who struggle an opportunity to hear thinking from a peer. Think-pair-share works well if partners are assigned before the lesson. This way, when the teacher directs students to think and then share, each child knows exactly whom to talk to. See this lesson's "Teacher Reflection" section on page 45 for more on the think-pair-share strategy.

A Child's Mind . . .

Do not be surprised if many students are unsure if 9 + 6 = 15. Conservation of number develops at different times for students. As students are exposed to more experiences with thinking about conservation ideas, they will move closer toward understanding.

Do a think-pair-share. Ask students to think of a number sentence that matches what they now see. Tell them to turn to a partner (seated next to them) and discuss their number sentence. Ask students to raise their hands when they are ready to answer.

5. Record *9 + 6 = 10 + 5*. Ask students for the sum of ten and five, then record *15* under the 10 + 5 sentence. Ask students, "Does nine plus six equal fifteen?" On the demonstration double ten-frame, move the counter back to re-create 9 + 6.

Count the counters to confirm that 9 + 6 does equal 15. Record *15* under 9 + 6:

9 + 6 = 10 + 5

15 = 15

Example 2: 9 + 4

6. Leaving some space between the previous number sentences, record *9 + 4*. Using the demonstration double ten-frame again, fill the first ten-frame with nine counters of one color and the second ten-frame with four counters of another color.

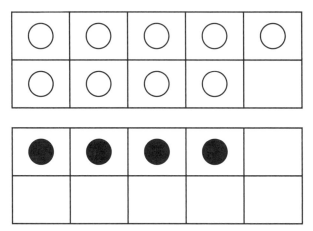

7. Ask students, "How can we make a ten to help us solve nine plus four?" Move one counter from the second ten-frame to the top ten-frame.

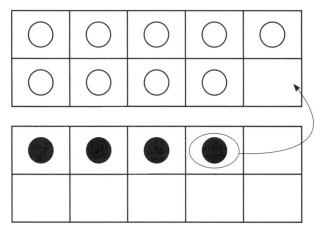

8. Ask students to think of a number sentence that matches what they now see.

9. Record *9 + 4 = 10 + 3*. Ask students for the sum of ten and three, then record *13* under the 10 + 3 sentence. Ask students, "Does nine plus four equal thirteen?" On the demonstration double ten-frame, move the counter back to re-create 9 + 4.

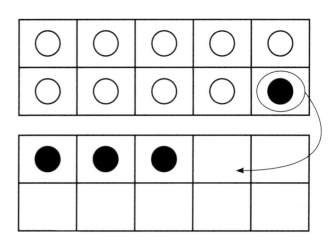

Count the counters to confirm that 9 + 4 does equal 13. Record *13* under 9 + 4. Your recording space may look like the following:

9 + 4 = 10 + 3

13 = 13

10. Direct students' attention to the number sentences you've recorded. Ask students to turn to their partners and discuss what they notice. Prompt (if necessary) by asking:

▶ What do you notice about the first number in the number sentences? How does it change?

▶ What do you notice about the second number in the number sentences? How does it change?

▶ Why are the sums the same when we add 9 + 6 and 10 + 5?

Example 3: 9 + 5

11. To begin to help students develop an internalized use of this strategy, write 9 + 5 on the board and ask students to think about what the double ten-frame would look like. Then ask what the new number sentence would be if they used ten to help them solve 9 + 5. Accept all answers before building 9 + 5 on the demonstration double ten-frame using one color for 9 and another color for 5 and moving the last counter from the second ten-frame to the first ten-frame to make a ten.

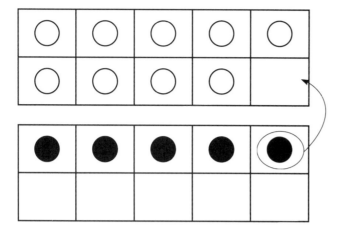

Ask students to think about a number sentence that matches what they now see.

12. Record *9 + 5 = 10 + 4*. Ask students for the sum of ten and four, then record *14* under the 10 + 4 sentence. Ask students, "Does nine plus five equal fourteen?" On the demonstration double ten-frame, move the counter back to re-create 9 + 5.

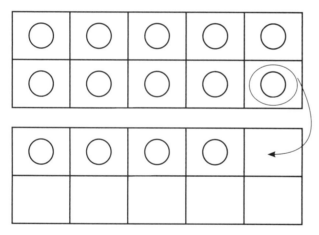

Count the counters to confirm that 9 + 5 does equal 14. Record 14 under the 9 + 5. Your recording space may look like the following:

$$9 + 5 = 10 + 4$$

$$14 = 14$$

13. Summarize by telling students that during the activity it will be important for them to think about what the new number sentence will be before making it on the ten-frame.

Teaching Tip

Repeat the whole-class routine *Adding Nine* several times before implementing Example 4.

Time Saver

As students are settling in for the day, ask the first two students who arrive to help with preparing the day's math materials. These students can count out groups of ten counters and place each group in a plastic sandwich bag. This makes it easy to distribute the counters when it comes time to do so. Alternatively, have each student count out a group of ten counters as soon as he or she enters the room. Once again, students can place their counters in plastic sandwich bags so you can easily distribute the materials when the time comes to do so.

Example 4: Students' Turn!

14. Let students know you would like them to work on a few addition problems with their partners. Explain that partners will receive one double ten-frame, two *Adding Nine* recording sheets (Reproducible 2), and twenty counters. Pass out the items.

15. To clarify directions, model at least the first problem on the *Adding Nine* recording sheet: $9 + 7 = 10 +$ _____. Ask students to fill the first ten-frame with nine counters of one color and the second ten-frame with seven counters of another color. Ask students, "How can we make a ten to help us solve the problem?" Direct students to move one counter from the second ten-frame to the first ten-frame. Ask students to write the new number sentence on their handouts. Give them time to complete this before recording $9 + 7 = 10 + 6$ on the board. Allow time for students to check their thinking. Ask if anyone has questions, then invite students to complete, in pairs, the *Adding Nine* recording sheet. See Figure R–5.1 for a sample completed recording sheet.

Summarize

16. When students are finished, begin a class discussion by recording *9 + 4* and displaying a double ten-frame. Do not fill the double ten-frame; instead explain to students that you would like them to visualize what the double ten-frame would look like if it were used to solve the problem. Ask them to think about how making a ten might help them solve 9 + 4. Have them turn to their partners to share their thinking. Call on volunteers to describe their thinking. Repeat with a few more *Adding Nine* problems.

17. On subsequent days, spend five to ten minutes reviewing *Adding Nine* problems by displaying the double ten-frame and recording

various *Adding Nine* problems. Ask students to think about how making a ten might help them solve each problem. Give students time to discuss their strategies.

Adding Nine

Directions

1. Look at the problem. Use counters to build the first number sentence on your double ten-frame.

2. Make a ten on your double ten-frame by rearranging the counters you've placed, and complete the second number sentence.

3. Figure out the sum. Record the sum for both sentences.

1. $9 + 7 = 10 +$ _6_
   $16 = 16$

2. $9 + 2 = 10 +$ _1_
   $11 = 11$

3. $9 + 8 = 10 +$ _7_
   $17 = 17$

4. $9 + 4 = 10 +$ _3_
   $13 = 13$

5. $9 + 6 = 10 +$ _5_
   $15 = 15$

6. $9 + 5 = 10 +$ _4_
   $14 = 14$

7. $9 + 1 = 10 +$ _0_
   $10 = 10$

8. $9 + 3 = 10 +$ _2_
   $12 = 12$

FIGURE R-5.1 After working with Emily on how to make a ten and record using the recording sheet, she was able to work independently

Adding Nine

Directions

1. Look at the problem. Use counters to build the first number sentence on your double ten-frame.

2. Make a ten on your double ten-frame by rearranging the counters you've placed, and complete the second number sentence.

3. Figure out the sum. Record the sum for both sentences.

1. $9 + 7 = 10 + \underline{6}$
   $\underline{16} = \underline{16}$

2. $9 + 2 = 10 + \underline{1}$
   $\underline{11} = \underline{11}$

3. $9 + 8 = 10 + \underline{7}$
   $\underline{17} = \underline{17}$

4. $9 + 4 = \underline{10} + \underline{3}$
   $\underline{13} = \underline{13}$

5. $9 + 6 = \underline{10} + \underline{5}$
   $\underline{15} = \underline{15}$

6. $9 + 5 = \underline{10} + \underline{4}$
   $\underline{14} = \underline{14}$

7. $9 + 1 = \underline{10} + \underline{1}$
   $\underline{10} = \underline{10}$

8. $9 + 3 = \underline{10} + \underline{2}$
   $\underline{12} = \underline{12}$

FIGURE R-5.2 Chloe quit using the ten-frame and counters because she could mentally use the Making Ten strategy

Extend Their Learning!

When students have completed the *Adding Nine* handout, consider the following two extensions.

Extension 1

Pass out a set of ten-frame cards to each pair of students. Ask students to find the ten-frame card with nine dots on it and place it faceup. The rest of the cards should be placed facedown in one pile. Explain to students that they must take turns with their partners. The first partner turns the top card on the pile over and adds the number to nine (referring to the card with nine dots). To help them add the cards, let students know they can use the double ten-frame or visualize the ten-frame. They should continue to think about how making a ten helps them solve the problem. When the first partner has added the two numbers, he should take the card he turned over (but leave the card with nine dots). The other partner then repeats the steps.

Extension 2

Ask students to turn their *Adding Nine* handouts over and write the addition facts for nine (i.e., 9 + 1 through 9 + 9). They should then solve them using what they know about ten. As students work, move from group to group and ask the key questions.

Assessment: Adding Nine

For an easy-to-implement assessment, record all the addition facts from 9 + 1 to 9 + 10 on individual note cards. Working with students individually, shuffle the cards and hand the pile to a student. Ask the student to flip through the cards and call out the sum for each fact. Use the *Adding Nine* assessment checklist (Reproducible 3) to formatively assess what the student knows and needs to work on.

Adding Nine Assessment Checklist

Adding 9 Fact	Knew Instantly or with a Small Amount of Thinking	Used a Strategy Like Making a Ten	Used a Counting Strategy Like Counting on or Counting All	Called Out the Wrong Answer (Record the child's answer in the box.)	Could Not Figure Out

FIGURE R-5.3 Reproducible 3: *Adding Nine* Assessment Checklist

Teacher Reflection

My *Adding Nine* Experiences

Think-Pair-Share

In my classroom, students have assigned seats when they come to the rug for whole-group learning. This way each child knows exactly where to go, no one saves a seat for a friend (thus making others feel badly), and no one runs up to the front to sit close to the teacher! I change their assigned seats monthly so students have the opportunity to sit beside other peers as well as rotate from the back to the front. Each time I make a new seating arrangement, I reassign think-pair-share partners. Because I use think-pair-share often, I want students to immediately know whom to talk to (versus looking around for someone). At the beginning of the year, I always model the appropriate way to think-pair-share. Students need to turn their bodies toward their partners and speak without interrupting each other. We practice this during the first six weeks of school by considering social questions like "What is a fun thing you did this weekend?" After they think-pair-share, I ask students to report what they heard from their partners to promote the idea of listening to each other.

Routine 6

Sums of More Than Ten

Overview

This four-part routine gives students opportunities to use and apply the strategy of making a ten to help them solve near-ten addition facts. In addition to developing basic fact fluency, the routine promotes the building of mental math skills through the visualization of ten-frames and number sentences.

Related Lessons

You might teach the following lessons first:

▶ G-6 *Collect Ten*

▶ R-5 *Adding Nine*

Consider this lesson as a follow-up:

▶ G-8 *Double Bank It!*

Key Questions

▶ How does knowing a combination of ten help you solve the new problem?

▶ How many counters do you see and how do you know?

Time

20 minutes per part (see page 63 for additional insights)

Materials

demonstration double ten-frame (see Reproducible D)

double ten-frame (Reproducible D), 1 per student or pair of students

Sums of More Than Ten Cards, Version 1 (Reproducible 4), 1 set per student or pair of students

Sums of More Than Ten recording sheet (Reproducible 6), 1 copy for each student

counters in two colors, 10 of each color for teacher and per student or pair of students

Teaching Directions

Part 1: Solving Facts That Have a Sum of One More Than Ten

1. Explain to students that the focus of this lesson is to use the combinations of ten that they know to help them solve addition facts with sums that are one more than ten.

Example 1: How 7 + 3 Can Help Us Solve 7 + 4

2. Ask students to think about how 7 + 3 can help them solve 7 + 4. Write 7 + 4 on the board.

3. Display a demonstration double ten-frame and fill the first ten-frame with seven counters of one color and the second ten-frame with four counters of the other color.

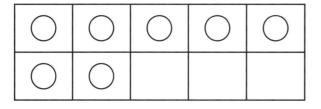

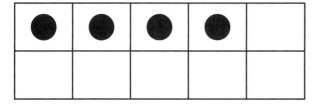

Ask students, "How many more counters are needed to fill the ten-frame that has seven counters on it?" When students say, "Three," take three counters from the second ten-frame and place them on the first ten-frame, thus completing the top frame.

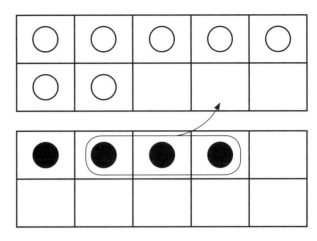

Technology Tip

Creating Ten-Frames on an Interactive Whiteboard

If an interactive whiteboard is available, create ten-frames by making two 5-by-2 tables. Create red and blue circles to be used as counters and apply the infinite cloner.

Differentiating Your Instruction

Think-pair-share allows all students time to process the question, think about an answer, and test out their thinking before having to speak in front of the whole class. This format also gives students who struggle an opportunity to hear thinking from a peer. Think-pair-share works well if partners are assigned before the lesson. This way, when the teacher directs students to think and then share, each child knows exactly whom to talk to. See R-5: Adding Nine's "Teacher Reflection" section on page 45 for more on the think-pair-share strategy.

Ask students, "How many counters are left on the second ten-frame?" When students say, "One," connect the action to the symbolic notation by recording $7 + 4 = 10 + 1$. As you record, explain that you split the four into three and one, so you could add three to the seven to make ten.

4. Do a think-pair-share. Ask students to quietly think about what they see on the demonstration double ten-frame. Ask them to think about the total number of counters. Then have students turn to their partners and discuss how they figured out the sum. Call on a few students to explain their thinking to the whole class. Some students might reply that they see ten and one more, which makes eleven. Others may reply that they see five and five and one more, which makes eleven.

5. Record $= 11$ under the $10 + 1$ and ask students if $7 + 4$ also equals 11. Confirm the sum by re-creating $7 + 4$ on the demonstration double ten-frame and counting the counters. Record 11 so it's now under both equations:

$$7 + 4 = 10 + 1$$
$$11 = 11$$

6. Summarize the strategy by asking students to explain to their partners how knowing $7 + 3 = 10$ can help them solve $7 + 4$. Record *7 + 3 = 10* and *7 + 4 = 11* like this:

$7 + 3 = 10$

$7 + 4 = 11$

7. Call on a few volunteers to explain their thinking to the class.

Examples of Student Thinking

"Seven plus four is really seven plus three with one extra."

"The four can be broken into a three and one so seven and three can be added first, then the one."

Example 2: How 8 + 2 Can Help Us Solve 8 + 3

8. Tell students that you now want them to think about how $8 + 2$ will help them solve $8 + 3$. Write *8 + 3* on the board.

9. Display the demonstration double ten-frame again and fill the first ten-frame with eight counters of one color and the second ten-frame with three counters of the other color.

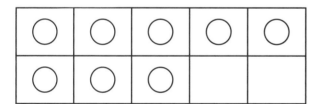

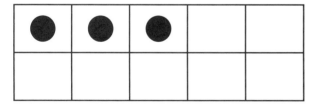

Ask students, "How many more counters are needed to fill the ten-frame that has eight counters on it?" When students say, "Two," take two counters from the second ten-frame and place them on the first ten-frame, thus completing the top frame.

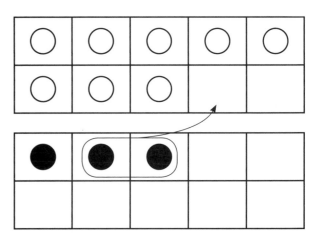

Ask students, "How many counters are left on the second ten-frame?" When students say, "One," connect the actions to the symbolic notation by recording *8 + 3 = 10 + 1*. As you record, explain that you split the three into two and one, so you could add two to the eight to make ten.

10. Ask students to quietly think about what they see on the demonstration double ten-frame. Ask them to think about the total number of counters. Then have students turn to their partners and discuss how they figured out the sum. Call on a few students to explain their thinking to the whole class.

11. Record = *11* under the 10 + 1 and ask students if 8 + 3 also equals 11. Confirm the sum by re-creating 8 + 3 on the demonstration double ten-frame and counting the counters. Record *11* so it's now under both equations:

    $$8 + 3 = 10 + 1$$

    $$11 = 11$$

12. Summarize the strategy by asking students to explain to their partners how knowing 8 + 2 = 10 can help them solve 8 + 3. Record *8 + 2 = 10* and *8 + 3 = 11* like this:

    $$8 + 2 = 10$$

    $$8 + 3 = 11$$

13. Call on a few volunteers to explain their thinking to the class.

Example 3: Solving 5 + 6

14. Point out to students that in the examples thus far, the number sentences have all started with the larger number. Now you would like them to think about number sentences that start with the smaller number first. Write *5 + 6 =* on the board.

15. On the demonstration double ten-frame, fill the first ten-frame with five counters of one color and the second ten-frame with six counters of the other color.

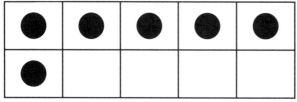

Ask students, "Do you want to fill the first ten-frame, which has five counters on it, or the second ten-frame, which has six counters on it? Think quietly about which one you'd like to fill." Then ask students to show a thumbs-up for the first ten-frame or a thumbs-down for the second ten-frame. Acknowledge that you saw thumbs pointed both ways and that both ways of thinking are acceptable.

16. Tell students you are going to model both ways, but first you will start by filling the top frame. Ask students, "How many counters are needed to fill the first ten-frame?" When students say, "Five," take five counters from the second ten-frame and place them on the first ten-frame, thus completing the top frame.

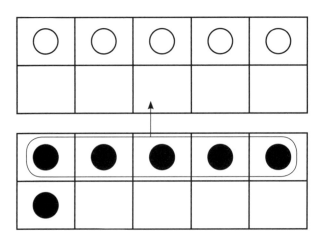

Ask students, "How many counters are left on the second ten-frame?" When students say, "One," connect the action to the symbolic notation by recording *5 + 6 = 10 + 1*. As you record, explain that you split the six into five and one, so you could add five to the five to make ten.

17. Do a think-pair-share. Ask students to quietly think about what they see on the demonstration double ten-frame. Ask them to think about the total number of counters. Then have students turn to their partners and discuss how they figured out the sum. Call on a few students to explain their thinking to the whole class.

18. Record *11* under both equations:

    5 + 6 = 10 + 1

    11 = 11

    If students need confirmation that 5 + 6 = 11, rebuild the equation on the demonstration double ten-frame and count the counters.

19. Summarize the strategy by asking students to explain to their partners how knowing 5 + 5 = 10 can help them solve 5 + 6. Record *5 + 5 = 10* and *5 + 6 = 11* like this:

    5 + 5 = 10

    5 + 6 = 11

20. Call on a few volunteers to explain their thinking to the class.

21. Now rebuild 5 + 6 on the demonstration double ten-frame and acknowledge that some students would like to fill the second ten-frame.

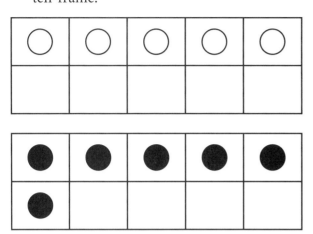

22. Ask students, "How many counters are needed to fill the ten-frame that has six counters on it?" When students say, "Four," take four counters from the first ten-frame and place them on the second ten-frame, thus completing the bottom frame.

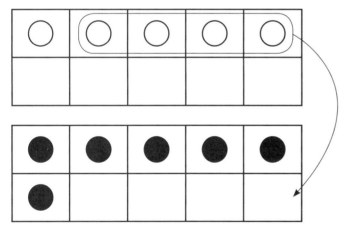

Ask students, "How many counters are left on the first ten-frame?" When students say, "One," connect the action to the symbolic notation by recording *5 + 6 = 1 + 10*. As you record, explain how the numbers in the second sentence connect to the counters on the frames.

23. Ask students to quietly think about what they see on the demonstration double ten-frame. Ask them to think about the total number of counters. Then have students

turn to their partners and discuss how they figured out the sum. Call on a few students to explain their thinking to the whole class.

24. Record *11* under both equations:

5 + 6 = 1 + 10

11 = 11

25. Ask students to look at both sets of number sentences for 5 + 6 and think about which strategy feels more comfortable—filling the first ten-frame or the second ten-frame. Allow a few students to volunteer their opinions.

26. Summarize by letting students know that sometimes it will feel more comfortable to make the first number a ten and sometimes it will feel more comfortable to make the second number a ten. The goal is for them be able to learn to add numbers efficiently.

27. Repeat this part of the routine a few times a month.

Part 2: Solving Facts That Have Sums of a Few More Than Ten

1. On another day, continue Part 2 of *Sums of More Than Ten*. Explain to students that the focus of this part of the routine is to use the combinations of ten they know to help them solve facts that have sums of a few more than ten.

Example 1: How 7 + 3 Can Help Us Solve 7 + 5

2. Ask students, "How can seven plus three help you solve seven plus five?" Write *7 + 5* on the board. Give students time to think.

3. Display the demonstration double ten-frame and fill the first ten-frame with seven counters of one color and the second ten-frame with five counters of the other color.

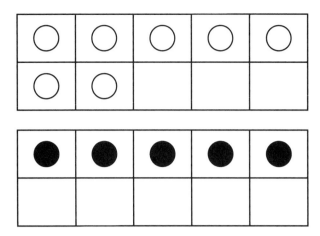

4. Ask students, "How many counters are needed to fill the ten-frame that has seven counters on it?" When students say, "Three," take three counters from the second ten-frame and place them on the first ten-frame, thus completing the top frame.

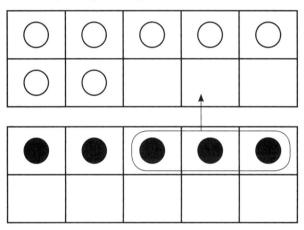

Ask students, "How many counters are left on the second ten-frame?" When students say, "Two," connect the action to the symbolic notation by recording $7 + 5 = 10 + 2$. As you record, explain that you split five into the amounts three and two so that you could fill the first ten-frame to make a ten.

5. Do a think-pair-share. Ask students to quietly think about what they see on the demonstration double ten-frame. Ask them to think about the total number of counters. Then have students turn to their partners and discuss how they figured out the sum. Call on a few students to explain their

thinking to the whole class. Some students might reply that they see ten and two more, which makes twelve. Others may reply that they see five and five and two more, which makes twelve.

6. Record *12* under both equations:

$$7 + 5 = 10 + 2$$

$$12 = 12$$

7. Summarize the strategy by asking students to explain to their partners how knowing $7 + 3 = 10$ can help them solve $7 + 5$. Record $7 + 3 = 10$ and $7 + 5 = 12$ like this:

$$7 + 3 = 10$$

$$7 + 5 = 12$$

8. Call on a few volunteers to explain their thinking to the class.

Examples of Student Thinking

"Seven plus five is really seven plus three with two extra."

"The five can be broken into a three and two, so seven and three can be added first, then the two."

Example 2: How 8 + 2 Can Help Us Solve 8 + 5

9. Ask students to think about how $8 + 2$ can help them solve $8 + 5$. Write *8 + 5* on the board. Give students time to think.

10. Using the demonstration double ten-frame, fill the first ten-frame with eight counters of one color and the second ten-frame with five counters of the other color.

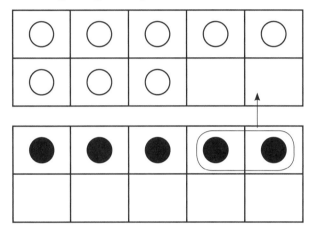

Ask students, "How many counters are needed to fill the ten-frame that has eight counters on it?" When students say, "Two," take two counters from the second ten-frame and place them on the first ten-frame, thus completing the top frame.

Ask students, "How many counters are left on the second ten-frame?" When students say, "Three," connect the action to the symbolic notation by recording *8 + 5 = 10 + 3*. As you record, explain how the numbers in the second sentence connect to the counters on the frames.

11. Ask students to quietly think about what they see on the demonstration double ten-frame. Ask them to think about the total number of counters. Then have students turn to their partners and discuss how they figured out the sum. Call on a few students to explain their thinking to the whole class.

12. Record *13* under both number sentences.

13. Summarize the strategy by asking students to explain to their partners how knowing 8 + 2 = 10 helps them solve 8 + 5. Record *8 + 2 = 10* and *8 + 5 =13* like this:

> *8 + 2 = 10*
>
> *8 + 5 = 13*

14. Call on a few volunteers to explain their thinking to the class.

15. Repeat this part of the routine a few times a month. Use equations such as 6 + 7, 8 + 4, 7 + 4, 8 + 6, and 8 + 7. Also repeat using the same equations to give students multiple experiences with the same numbers.

Part 3: Sums More Than Ten Activity

1. Introduce the activity that complements this routine. Let students know this activity can be worked on alone or with a partner. Show students a stack of cards made from the *Sums of More Than Ten Cards, Version 1* reproducible (Reproducible 4). Place the cards in a pile and turn the top card over. Build the corresponding number sentence on the demonstration double ten-frame using two colors of counters. Show students the *Sums of More Than Ten Recording Sheet* (Reproducible 6) and on the board, set up blanks like those shown on the recording sheet:

$$\underline{\hspace{1.5cm}} + \underline{\hspace{1.5cm}} = \underline{\hspace{1.5cm}} + \underline{\hspace{1.5cm}}$$

$$\underline{\hspace{2.5cm}} = \underline{\hspace{2.5cm}}$$

Fill in the first two blanks with the number sentence from *the card you turned over.*

$$\underline{\hspace{0.5cm}7\hspace{0.5cm}} + \underline{\hspace{0.5cm}5\hspace{0.5cm}} = \underline{\hspace{1.5cm}} + \underline{\hspace{1.5cm}}$$

$$\underline{\hspace{2.5cm}} = \underline{\hspace{2.5cm}}$$

2. Explain to students that for this activity they will need to use what they know about making a ten. Ask students, "What needs to be done to make a ten?" Move the appropriate counters to make a ten on the demonstration double ten-frame. Ask students, "What combination of ten helps solve this problem? How many counters are left over?" Fill in the next two blanks on the board.

$$\underline{\hspace{0.5cm}7\hspace{0.5cm}} + \underline{\hspace{0.5cm}5\hspace{0.5cm}} = \underline{\hspace{0.4cm}10\hspace{0.4cm}} + \underline{\hspace{0.5cm}2\hspace{0.5cm}}$$

$$\underline{\hspace{2.5cm}} = \underline{\hspace{2.5cm}}$$

Teaching Tip

Why Two Versions of Cards?
Students need repeated experiences applying how making a ten can help them efficiently learn their facts. Once students have completed *Sums of More Than Ten Cards, Version 1* (Reproducible 4), I ask them to work with the cards from *Sums of More Than Ten Cards, Version 2* (Reproducible 5) on another day.

3. Ask students to think about what they see on the demonstration double ten-frame. What is the total number of counters? Record the sum for each side of the equation.

$$\underline{\quad 7 \quad} + \underline{\quad 5 \quad} = \underline{\quad 10 \quad} + \underline{\quad 2 \quad}$$
$$\underline{\qquad 12 \qquad} = \underline{\qquad 12 \qquad}$$

4. Tell students they will turn over the next *Sums of More Than Ten* card and build the number sentence on their double ten-frame, then record it on their copy of the recording sheet. They will work to make a ten and record a number sentence to match their thinking. Finally, they will record the sum.

5. Pass out the *Sums of More Than Ten* cards and recording sheets. Make sure each student (or pair of students) has ten counters of one color and ten counters of another color. If you choose to let students work with in pairs, explain that each student will write on his or her own recording sheet but will share a double ten-frame, counters, and a set of *Sums of More Than Ten* cards with a partner. Model one round with a partner so students understand how to work together.

Part 4: Visualizing Sums of More Than Ten

1. Explain to students that you would like them to begin visualizing the make-a-ten strategy in their minds. Ask them to mentally picture the double ten-frame. Write *8 + 3* on the board and ask students, "How can making a ten in your mind help you solve eight plus three?" Encourage students to picture what this addition problem would look like on a double ten-frame.

2. Give students time to think before asking them to discuss ideas with their partners. Call on a volunteer to explain her thinking; while she does, connect her words to the symbolic representation. Here's an example of what a student might share and how you could model her thinking:

Time Saver

As students are settling in for the day, ask the first two students who arrive to help with preparing the day's math materials. These students can count out groups of ten counters in two different colors and place each group of twenty in a plastic sandwich bag. This makes it easy to distribute the counters when it comes time to do so. Alternatively, have each student count out a group of ten counters in two different colors as soon as he or she enters the room. Once again, students can place their counters in plastic sandwich bags so you can easily distribute the materials when the time comes to do so.

A Child's Mind . . .

Whether students work with partners or alone, they need to see the activity modeled and how to record using the recording sheet. Model the directions and consider writing the directions on the board.

Teaching Tip

Envisioning the Double Ten-Frame
It's helpful to display or pass out double ten-frames so students can see the frame. They will still have to mentally visualize 8 + 3, but the frame will support their thinking of making a ten.

Example of Student Thinking

"When I think of eight plus three, I can take two from the three and make the eight a ten. Then I have one left over, and ten and one is eleven."

$8 + 3 =$

$8 + 2 + 1 =$

$8 + 2 = 10$

$10 + 1 = 11$

3. Ask students if they have another way of describing how making a ten can help them solve 8 + 3.

4. Next write *4 + 7* on the board and ask students, "How can making a ten in your mind help you solve four plus seven?" Encourage students to picture what this addition problem would look like on a double ten-frame.

5. Give students time to think before asking them to discuss ideas with their partners. Call on a volunteer to explain his thinking; while he does, connect his words to the symbolic representation. Here are some examples of what a student might share and how you could record his thinking:

Examples of Student Thinking

"When I think of four plus seven, I can take three from the four and make the seven a ten. Then I have one left over, and ten and one is eleven."

$4 + 7 =$

$3 + 1 + 7 =$

$3 + 7 = 10$

$10 + 1 = 11$

"When I think of four plus seven, I can take six from the seven and make the four a ten. Then I have one left over, and ten and one is eleven."

$4 + 7 =$

$4 + 6 + 1 =$

$4 + 6 = 10$

$10 + 1 = 11$

6. Ask students if they have another way of describing how making a ten can help them solve $7 + 4$.

7. Continue to build students' mental math skills by repeating the procedure on subsequent days during the routines portion of your math class.

Teacher Reflection

My *Sums of More Than Ten* Experiences
Moving Counters

During this routine, I move from left to right and top to bottom when filling in the demonstration double ten-frame with counters. I fill the double ten-frame in this manner for consistency. I recognize that numbers can be built various ways on the double ten-frames, but I want students to focus on making a ten and eventually internalize how to use making a ten to solve basic facts. I've found that if I change how I build nine counters, for example, some students focus on looking at the different ways to see the nine. Thinking about different ways to see a number is the purpose of the *Look, Quick!* (see R-1) and *Make the Number* (see R-2) routines, but not of this routine.

When making the ten, I consistently move the counters up from right to left so that the leftovers on the double ten-frame are from left to right.

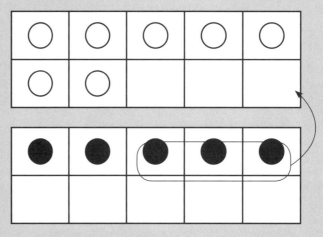

Again, I recognize that any of the counters could be moved to make a ten; however, I want the leftovers to be grouped together starting at the top left corner. When students work independently or in pairs, I observe students moving counters to make a ten in a variety of ways. I do not make them follow my same pattern as long as they are able to make sense of moving their counters and finding the sum.

Repeating the Routine

I find this routine to be most successful when I repeat Parts 1 and 2 several times a week for a few months. I go through approximately two problems each time I implement this routine. The repeated experience of thinking about making a ten helps students use the strategy. By the time I ask students to engage in the activity in Part 3, they have seen how I record making a ten and they have discussed making ten several times. I implement Part 4 during the remainder of the year, approximately two to three times a month for repeated practice.

Games Using Ten-Frames

Why these math games?

I chose the math games featured in this section because they are outstanding at encouraging students to rely on strategy or thoughtful decisions. The games offer students an opportunity to work with their peers, discuss math in the context of an enjoyable activity, and practice skills (both skills that are newly acquired and those that were taught previously in the year).

This section opens with three memory games. Memory games increase students' concentration level and encourage them to pay attention in their search for a matching pair of cards. *More or Less* (G-4) builds an understanding of inclusion and *more than* or *less than* ideas. Additionally, *More or Less, Part 2* (also G-4) explores combinations of ten. *Make Five* (G-5) and *Collect Ten* (G-6) give students practice looking for and learning the combinations of five and ten. *Bank It!* (G-7) and *Double Bank It!* (G-8) focus on comparing numbers and equations. *Race to 20* (G-9) builds students' understanding of landmark numbers as they work on number strings up to twenty.

When should I teach with math games?

Finding time to give students repeated opportunities to play games can be challenging but rewarding. Once you've taken time to introduce students to a particular game, played the game during math time, and had an opportunity to discuss the content and strategies, you can repeatedly use that game in stations, or centers, or when there is extra time during the day. This extra time might be in the mornings, when students are arriving and putting away their backpacks, during rainy-day recesses, or during transition times (if there is time left before lunch or fine arts, for example).

Do I need to prepare materials in advance for these math games?

Ten-Frame Cards, Ten-Frames, and Double Ten-Frames

Most of the games in this section require the use of ten-frame cards (Reproducible B). Before the school year begins, I recommend making four sets of the ten-frame cards for the average number of students you normally have in your classroom. (A set of ten-frame cards is four copies of Reproducible B, for a total of forty cards.) Creating enough sets for each student ensures that there will be enough for all partners to play games at the same time. Copy each set of cards on colored paper or card stock. Then label the back of each set with a different letter or sticker. For example, the first set of ten-frame cards might be labeled *A* or have a yellow smiley-face sticker. This way, when a card is misplaced, one can simply check the back to match it with the appropriate set. When you are finished creating the cards, laminate them to ensure extended use. Store each set in a plastic sandwich bag (consider asking parents—your school's PTO or PTA—or friends to donate the bags or money for the bags).

Several games call for the use of a ten-frame (Reproducible A) or double ten-frame (Reproducible D). Like the ten-frame cards, copy these on colored card stock and laminate. Create enough for each student to have their own ten-frame and double ten-frame.

Counters

If a game requires counters, ask students who come to the room early to begin counting out the needed supplies and placing them in containers or plastic sandwich bags. If you have enough materials, keep sets of twenty counters in plastic bags (quart-size freezer bags work best) at all times.

How do I manage my classroom during math games?

It's important to manage students during game play, and there are many techniques for doing so. It is the teacher's role to set clear expectations and supervise students while they are playing games. Many of the issues that arise when students are playing games can be avoided via careful preplanning. Following are a few helpful tips.

Assigning Partners

Assigning partners can be awkward for students, especially when they are assigned to play with someone whom they consider to not be a friend. Prepare students for assigned partners by setting clear expectations. Make it a goal from the beginning for students to have many different partners during the school year. Explicitly state that it is inappropriate to show upset expressions or say unkind words. Discuss disciplinary actions as necessary. Finally, let students know the length of time they will be expected to work with their partners, such as thirty minutes.

Letting Students Choose Partners

After the year is well under way and you have clearly established routines for playing games, consider allowing students to choose their partners. One structured way to start this is to ask a few students as they arrive in the morning, "Whom would you like to play a game with during math?" Start a list of those who choose partners (and their corresponding partners). For those who do not choose a partner, assign them one and include them on the list. During math, read or post the list of partnerships without stating who picked their partners. This way, students won't feel like they were picked last.

Additionally, when you give students the opportunity to choose partners, it's helpful to discuss with the class that sometimes best friends do not make the best game partners. Encouraging students to choose game partners that they work well with helps students become responsible for their own learning. Once again, setting clear expectations is crucial; explain that if students choose someone and end up not following directions or working well together, you will choose new partners for them.

Playing at Desks Versus the Floor

During the first six to nine weeks of school, most games should be played at students' desks for the simple reason that students most likely are used to sitting and working at their desks. Once routines are in place and students are demonstrating appropriate game-playing behavior, you might choose to move them to the floor. If students act silly or are not following directions, warn them that if they don't behave, they will have to move back to their desks and continue to play the game there.

An advantage of playing games at desks is that you can see students better than if they are seated on the floor. On the other hand, it is easier for dice or counters to fall on the floor from desks, thus delaying game play.

There are also advantages to playing games on the floor. Students are more relaxed sitting on the floor and tend to sit either face-to-face or elbow-to–elbow. In addition, materials can be easier for students to use on the floor.

Managing the Use of Game Pieces

It's typical in any primary classroom to find game pieces left over on the floor from a previously played game. During the beginning of the year, emphasize cleanup by having students check around them, under them, and near them for any stray materials.

Primary-aged students are notorious for following teachers around the room, letting them know they found an item. To help build autonomy, at the beginning of the year, hold up a frequently lost game piece, ask students to be problem solvers, and encourage them to think quietly about where the item goes. Give students time to share their thoughts with their partners, then hold a class discussion about what to do when misplaced or lost items are found. This type of discussion encourages students to take ownership of their classroom and put away these items on their own.

> ### ⓘ Teaching Tip
>
> #### Managing the Use of Dice
> Using dice can be problematic if students are rolling them across the entire floor or throwing them across tables. To prevent such scenarios, give each group of students a 6-by-6-inch square of soft foam (the kind you line kitchen cabinets with) and tell students they will lose their turn if they roll the dice off the foam. Setting such parameters decreases chaos (rolling—and in some cases, flying!—dice) and maintains control in the classroom.

Keep in mind that for this approach to work, materials need to be readily accessible to students. Keep manipulatives in containers that are low enough for students to reach. Setting up a container or large plastic bag and labeling it "I'm lost!" for lost items helps students know what to do when they find a misplaced game piece but are unsure of where it belongs. At the end of the day or week you can place these lost items in their proper place.

Why is it important to model math games?

For primary-aged students, modeling how to play a math game is critical to the success they will have while playing it. I find it best to seat students on the floor while modeling a game. Have students sit on the perimeter of the whole-group area, and place the game materials in the center. This ensures that each student has a chance to see and hear what is going on while also being in close proximity to the teacher. Simultaneously, you can quickly tell who is and is not paying attention and redirect behavior as necessary.

It helps to assign places for students to sit in the whole-group area; doing so alleviates students' desire to run to the front of the area or save a seat for a friend. Consider also strategically placing students who would benefit from sitting in the front or closer to the teacher.

There is more to modeling a game than simply performing the instructions. It's important that students see how to behave while playing a game. Emphasize the following three behaviors when modeling: waiting patiently for your turn, appropriately passing game pieces to your partner, and winning or losing gracefully.

It is also important for students to hear others thinking about the game. While modeling the game, the teacher should be asking the key questions so important mathematical ideas are discussed.

Waiting Patiently for Your Turn

To model waiting patiently for your turn, remind students of what their role is while they wait. They might need to be checking their partner's work or checking their own work from previous rounds. Waiting patiently does not mean repeatedly telling your partner what to do or giving your partner the answer; emphasize that such actions take the learning away from the partner. (On the other hand, if your partner asks for help, you may help!)

Teaching Tip

Brainstorming How to Win or Lose Gracefully

While my students were playing math games once, I overheard a student who won tell his partner, "Good game! You'll probably win next time." I took note of this and mentioned it to the whole class during closing that day. I emphasized how nice it was to say this. I asked students to think of other kind phrases they could say when a game was over. As students volunteered their thoughts, I recorded the phrases on chart paper. I titled the chart "What to Say When a Game Is Over" and taped it to the classroom wall. Later in the year, a physical education coach told me that she had overheard my students saying these very lines to each other during kickball!

Appropriately Passing Game Pieces to Your Partner

Passing dice or cards to your partner may seem trivial but can quickly turn into an argument. Constant teacher modeling of the appropriate way to pass game pieces will make this act second nature to students.

Winning or Losing Gracefully

Winning and losing gracefully is a crucial life skill to acquire; it's important that this is developed during a child's foundational years. At the beginning of modeling a game, tell students that someone will win and someone will not win *this time*. Explain to students that they have a choice on how to react; whether they win or lose, their first statement should be "Good game." Note that having students play two against two can also help them feel more comfortable during competitive games.

What should I do while students are playing games?

While games are being played, teachers should observe students; make note of what students write on their recording sheets; ask key questions to extend students' learning and assess their understanding; and work with small groups when issues arise.

Using Recording Sheets

Recording sheets can serve both as formative assessment and summative assessment. Having students record their thinking while playing games is a valuable way to get insight into students' understandings. Before introducing a recording sheet, make sure students are familiar with the game and have played it several times. Don't forget to model how to complete the recording sheet before handing it out to students. Once students have started the game and are using their recording sheets, move around the room, taking note of what students are writing down. Ask students questions about what they have recorded. Additionally, collect and review students' recording sheets to gain insight for planning next steps for the class or small groups of students.

Most teachers are required to indicate student understanding by assigning grades or checking off indicators. Recording sheets can serve as summative assessments when you need to assign a grade.

Finally, whether you use recording sheets to plan future lessons or indicate what has been learned, you'll find them helpful when discussing students' understandings with parents and administrators.

Game 1

Dot Card Memory

Math Matters!

Subitizing

The ability to glance at a group of objects and quickly see how many there are without counting them one by one. (See *Math Matters: Understanding the Math You Teach, Grades K–8, Second Edition* by Suzanne H. Chapin and Art Johnson, © 2006 Math Solutions.)

Time

20 minutes

Materials

ten-frame cards (Reproducible B), 1 set per pair of students

dot cards (Reproducible E), 1 set per pair of students

Extension

ten-frame cards (Reproducible B), 1 set per pair of students

blank cards, 10 per pair of students

Overview

In this memory game, students subitize to match quantities on dot cards to quantities on ten-frame cards. Subitizing is the ability to see groups of objects. Being able to subitize is an important aspect of number sense that students develop through repeated experiences. Using the extension, students gain experience creating their own dot cards and have an opportunity to create and organize groups of dots.

Related Lesson

You might teach the following lesson first:

▶ R-1 Look, Quick!

Key Questions

▶ How can you figure out how many dots are on the card?

▶ How did you see the arrangements of dots?

▶ Is there another way to see the arrangement of dots?

▶ The two cards you turned over do not match. Which number is more? Which number is less?

▶ The two cards you turned over match. What number is one more than the cards you matched? What number is one less than the cards you matched?

Teaching Directions

1. Model the game first. To start, display the dot card with seven dots and tell students the goal is to figure out the number of dots on the card by looking for groups of dots they can see, rather than counting each dot.

2. Model a response: "I see a group of four and a group of three. Together, four and three is seven."

   Encourage multiple ways of seeing the same total on the dot card by asking students, "Is there another way to see the arrangement of dots?" Call on a few students to explain how they see the arrangement of dots.

3. Now explain to students that the next step is to find the ten-frame card with seven dots. Remind students that looking for groups is possible on the ten-frame cards too. Display the ten-frame card with seven dots. Tell students you were able to quickly see the card had seven dots because you saw a group of five dots in the top row and two more in the next row. Encourage multiple ways of seeing the same total on the ten-frame card by asking students, "Is there another way to see the arrangement of dots?" Call on a few students to explain how they see the arrangement of dots.

4. Give students another opportunity to practice looking for groups of dots on the ten-frame cards. Show the ten-frame card with nine dots. Ask students, "How can you figure out how many dots are on the card?"

Examples of Student Thinking

"I saw one less than ten."

"I saw five dots on the top row and four on the next row. I then added those together."

"I counted the dots by twos."

5. Use the game directions to further model the game with a student volunteer. Make sure to ask students if they have any questions before turning the game over to them.

6. Pass out one set of ten-frame cards and one set of dot cards to each pair of students.

7. As students play the game, circulate and ask questions (refer to the key questions).

Dot Card Memory

Objective

Players try to match the quantity on the dot card they turn over with the quantity on the ten-frame card they turn over. The winner is the player with the most cards.

Materials

1 set of ten-frame cards and 1 set of dot cards for each pair of players

Directions

1. Working in pairs, players shuffle all the cards and then place them facedown, forming a 4-by-5 array.

2. Player A turns over one card and reports the number of dots on it, then explains how he or she figured out how many dots are on the card.

3. Player A then turns over another card in the array.

   ▶ If the quantities match, Player A takes the two cards and places them in a pile next to him or her. Player A's turn is over.

   ▶ If the quantities do not match, Player A must give Player B time to see the two cards before turning them back over in the array. Player A's turn is over.

4. It is now Player B's turn. Player B repeats Steps 2 and 3.

5. Play continues until all the ten-frame cards have been matched to the dot cards.

6. The winner is the player with the most cards.

Differentiating Your Instruction

Modifying the Directions

If students are new to playing memory-type games or are struggling to remember where cards are placed, modify the directions so that cards are placed in two 2-by-5 arrays—one containing only ten-frame cards, the other containing only dot cards. Ask students to turn over one card from each array, thus ensuring they will always turn over a ten-frame card and a dot card.

Homework

For homework, you can send materials and game directions home with a note attached asking the parent and child to play the game three times.

Extend Their Learning!

Have students create their own dot cards. Distribute ten blank cards to each pair of students and ask them to draw their own dot arrangements for the numbers one through ten. Before students create their own dot arrangements, discuss the importance of drawing the dots in an arrangement with easy-to-see groups. Fill in a demonstration blank card with dots that are scattered in no particular order. Give students an opportunity to see the difficulty of looking for groups of dots on the demonstration card.

When pairs have finished creating their own dot cards, have them play the game using their dot cards mixed in with the ten-frame cards. Pairs of students can also trade their sets of dot cards with other pairs to play a new *Dot Card Memory* game.

Numeral Memory

Overview

In this memory game, students gain valuable practice in matching numerals with the corresponding quantities. The purpose of the game is to give students experience seeing ten-frame cards with dots and learning to look for ways to group the dots to determine the total, rather than always counting each dot one at a time.

Related Lessons

Consider these lessons as a follow-up:

▶ G-1 Dot Card Memory

▶ G-3 Computation Memory

Key Questions

▶ What do you think the ten-frame card that matches the numeral card you turned over will look like? How many squares will be *empty* on the ten-frame card?

▶ What strategies do you have for remembering where cards are located?

▶ The two cards you turned over do not match. Which number is more? Which number is less?

▶ The two cards you turned over match. What number is one more than the cards you matched? What number is one less than the cards you matched?

Time

10 minutes

Materials

ten-frame cards (Reproducible B),
1 set per pair of students

numeral cards (Reproducible F),
1 set per pair of students

Teaching Directions

1. Model the game first. Refer to the teaching directions for *Dot Card Memory* (see G-1 in this section of the book). This game is similar but uses numeral cards instead of dot cards.

2. Use the game directions to further model the game with a student volunteer. Make sure to ask students if they have any questions before turning the game over to them.

3. Pass out one set of ten-frame cards and one set of numeral cards to each pair of students.

4. As students play the game, circulate and ask questions (refer to the key questions).

Numeral Memory

Objective

Players try to match the numeral card they turn over with the corresponding quantity on the ten-frame card they turn over. The winner is the player with the most cards.

Materials

1 set of ten-frame cards and 1 set of numeral cards for each pair of players

Directions

1. Working in pairs, players shuffle all the cards and place them facedown, forming a 4-by-5 array.

2. Player A turns over one card.

   ▶ If it is a numeral card, Player A uses his or her fingers to show his or her partner the number of dots on a ten-frame card that would match.

   ▶ If it is a ten-frame card, Player A shows his or her partner the matching numeral by tracing the numeral in the air or on the palm of his or her hand.

3. Player A then turns over another card in the array.

   ▶ If the quantities match, Player A takes the two cards and places them in a pile next to him or her. Player A's turn is over.

   ▶ If the quantities do not match, Player A must give Player B time to see the two cards before turning them back over in the array. Player A's turn is over.

4. It is now Player B's turn. Player B repeats Steps 2 and 3.

5. Play continues until all the ten-frame cards have been matched to the numeral cards.

6. The winner is the player with the most cards.

Differentiating Your Instruction

Modifying the Directions

If students are new to playing memory-type games or are struggling to remember where cards are placed, modify the directions so that cards are placed in two 2-by-5 arrays—one containing only ten-frame cards and the other containing only numeral cards. Ask students to turn over one card from each pile, thus ensuring they will always turn over a ten-frame card and a numeral card.

Homework

For homework, you can send materials and game directions home with a note attached asking the parent and child to play the game three times.

Game 3
Computation Memory

Differentiating Your Instruction

Computation Cards

Computation card Sets A, B, and C are designed so that a teacher can differentiate. Some students will benefit from working solely with the addition cards. Others will need more of a challenge and find the addition and subtraction cards suitable. To further customize the game to fit the range of learners in your classroom, provide materials for students to create their own computation cards.

Time

10 minutes

Materials

ten-frame cards (Reproducible B), 1 set per pair of students

computation cards (Reproducibles G–I), 1 set (equaling 1–10) per pair of students—choose Set A (all addition), B (all subtraction), or C (a mixture of addition and subtraction)

Extension

ten-frame cards (Reproducible B), 1 set per pair of students

blank cards, 10 per pair of students

Overview

In this memory game, students practice their basic addition and subtraction facts by matching number sentences (on computation cards) with a total (on ten-frame cards). To extend their learning, you can give students the opportunity to create their own computation cards. The game is recommended for students who have been introduced to written number sentences and are practicing basic addition and subtraction facts.

Related Lesson

Consider these lessons as a follow-up:

▶ G-4 More or Less

▶ G-5 Make Five

Key Questions

▶ What number sentence would be equal to the quantity on this ten-frame card?

▶ You turned over two computation cards. Which number sentence equals more? Which number sentence equals less?

▶ You found a match. What other number sentences would be equal to the quantity on the ten-frame card?

Teaching Directions

1. Model the game first. Refer to the teaching directions for *Dot Card Memory* (see G-1 in this section of the book). This game is similar but uses computation cards instead of dot cards.

2. Use the game directions to further model the game with a student volunteer. Make sure to ask students if they have any questions before turning the game over to them.

3. Pass out one set of ten-frame cards and one set of computation cards to each pair of students.

4. As students play the game, circulate and ask questions (refer to the key questions).

Computation Memory

Objective

Players try to match the quantity on the ten-frame card they turn over with the value of the computation card they turn over. The winner is the player with the most cards.

Materials

1 set of ten-frame cards and 1 set of computation cards (equaling 1–10) for each pair of players

Directions

1. Working in pairs, players shuffle all the cards and place them facedown, forming a 4-by-5 array.

2. Player A turns over one card.

   ❯ If it is a computation card, Player A solves the equation and tells his or her partner the ten-frame card quantity he or she is looking for.

   ❯ If it is a ten-frame card, Player A tells his or her partner a number sentence that would be equal to the quantity on the ten-frame card.

3. Player A then turns over another card in the array.

   ❯ If the quantities match, Player A takes the two cards and places them in a pile next to him or her. Player A's turn is over.

   ❯ If the quantities do not match, Player A must give Player B time to see the two cards before turning them back over in the array. Player A's turn is over.

4. It is now Player B's turn. Player B repeats Steps 2–3.

5. Play continues until all the ten-frame cards have been matched to the computation cards.

6. The winner is the player with the most cards.

Homework

For homework, you can send materials and game directions home with a note attached asking the parent and child to play the game three times.

Extend Their Learning!

Have students create their own computation cards. Distribute ten blank cards to each pair of students and ask them to create one number sentence that is equal to each ten-frame card.

When pairs have created their own computation cards, have them play the game using their computation cards mixed in with the ten-frame cards. Pairs of students can also trade their sets of computation cards with other pairs to play a new *Computation Memory* game.

At the end of the game, ask students to record on a piece of paper the number sentence that matches the computation cards and ten-frame cards that they picked up. Students' recordings are helpful in confirming that students are adding correctly and also in giving students additional practice writing number sentences.

Game 4

More or Less

Time

20–30 minutes

Materials

demonstration ten-frame (see Reproducible A)

ten-frame (Reproducible A), 1 per pair of students

spinner (Reproducible 7), 1 for the teacher and 1 per pair of students

More or Less recording sheet (Reproducible 8), 1 copy for the teacher and 1 copy per student

counters, 10 for the teacher and 10 per pair of students

dice labeled 0–5, 2 for the teacher and 2 per pair of students

Overview

In this three-part game, students use a ten-frame to develop an understanding of inclusion and informally gain opportunities to consider *more than* and *less than* ideas. In Part 1, players roll two dice and build the sum of the two dice on their ten-frame. After students are familiar with Part 1, they move to Part 2, in which they use a spinner and recording sheet to create and record combinations of ten. Finally, Part 3 provides students the opportunity to summarize their thinking and learning from playing the game. I recommend that students play Part 1 for several days before introducing Part 2, with Part 3 following shortly thereafter.

Related Lesson

Consider this lesson as a follow-up:

▶ G-6 Collect Ten

Key Questions

▶ Does the ten-frame need "more or less" counters?

▶ How did you find the sum of the two dice?

▶ How did you think about putting "more or less" counters on the ten-frame?

Teaching Directions

Part 1: Building Sums

1. Explain to students that they will be playing a game using two dice and a ten-frame. The ten-frame is their game board. Display the demonstration ten-frame.

2. Ask a student volunteer to help you model the game for the class. Ask her to roll the two dice and call out the numbers rolled. Then ask her to add the two numbers in her head but not say the answer. Give everyone time to quietly think of the sum. Ask the volunteer, "What is the sum? Please take the number of counters equal to the sum and place them on the demonstration ten-frame."

3. Thank the volunteer student and ask her to pass the dice back to you. Roll the dice and call out the numbers rolled. Ask the students to quietly add the numbers and raise their hands when they know the sum. Call on several students to share their addition strategies.

4. Direct students' attention to the demonstration ten-frame and ask them, "To get to the new sum, do we need to add more counters to the ten-frame or do we need to take some counters off it?" Give students time to talk to partners, then ask the class to whisper whether the demonstration ten-frame needs "more or less" counters.

5. Ask a few students to volunteer explaining what they would do to the demonstration ten-frame to get to the new sum. Build the new sum on the demonstration ten-frame.

6. Pass the dice back to the student volunteer and allow her to take another turn. Tell her, "Please roll the two dice and call out the numbers rolled." Then ask her to add the two numbers. Ask the volunteer, "How did you find the sum of the two dice? Does the ten-frame need 'more or less' counters?" Once

Teaching Tip

Supporting ELLs

If necessary, or to support English language learners, introduce the word *sum* by writing it for the class to see, reading the word, and defining it for the students: "When we put two amounts together, we call that number the sum." (See *Supporting English Language Learners in Math Class, Grades K–2* by Rusty Bresser, Kathy Melanese, and Christine Sphar, © 2009 Math Solutions.)

A Child's Mind . . .

When students discuss their strategies, you will likely hear them saying they counted all the dots on the dice, counted on from one number, or just knew the fact. All ways of thinking should be accepted.

A Child's Mind . . .

In explaining what they would do, some students will want to clear the entire ten-frame and rebuild the new sum; others will want to add or subtract one at a time until they reach the new sum; yet others will know to add or subtract a specific number to reach the new sum. All ways of thinking should be accepted.

Teaching Tip

Passing the Dice

By asking students to pass the dice, you are modeling the appropriate behavior expected of them during the game. Also, encouraging students to pass the dice in a friendly manner instead of grabbing the dice will ensure fewer disagreements.

Time Saver

As students are settling in for the day, ask the first two students who arrive to help with preparing the day's math materials. These students can count out groups of ten counters for each pair of students and place each group in a plastic sandwich bag. This makes it easy to distribute the counters when it comes time to do so. Alternatively, have one student from each pair count out a group of ten counters as soon as he or she enters the room. Once again, students can place their counters in plastic sandwich bags so you can easily distribute the materials when the time comes to do so.

the volunteer has answered and moved the counters accordingly, ask her to pass the dice back to you.

7. Use the game directions to further model the game with students. Make sure to ask students if they have any questions before turning the game over to them.

8. Pass out one ten-frame, two dice, and ten counters to each pair of students.

9. As students play the game, circulate and ask questions (refer to the key questions).

More or Less, Part 1

Objective

In this cooperative activity, players roll two dice and build the sum on a ten-frame.

Materials

1 ten-frame, 2 dice, and 10 counters for each pair of players

Directions

1. Player A rolls the dice and calls out the numbers rolled. Player A then adds the two numbers and calls out the sum. Thirdly, Player A places the number of counters equal to the sum on the ten-frame.

2. Player A passes the dice to Player B. Player B rolls the dice and calls out the numbers rolled. Player B then adds the two numbers, calls out the sum, and repositions the counters as necessary on the ten-frame so that they equal the sum.

3. Players continue taking turns, adding or removing counters from the ten-frame as needed to match the sum of the dice rolled.

Homework

For homework, you can send materials and game directions home with a note attached asking the parent and child to play the game for ten to fifteen minutes.

Teaching Directions

Part 2: Recording Combinations of Ten

1. Remind students of what they did in Part 1. Tell them that they will be adding on to Part 1 of the game.

2. Ask a student volunteer to help you model Part 2 of the game with the class. Ask him to spin the spinner and call out the number it lands on. Then ask him to place that number of counters on the demonstration ten-frame.

3. Introduce the *More or Less* recording sheet (Reproducible 8). Explain to students that after they spin, they will need to fill in their recording sheets. In the first blank on their recording sheets, they need to record the number of squares with counters on their ten-frame. In the second blank, they need to record the number of squares without counters (empty squares) on their ten-frame. Then they add those numbers together to find the sum. Model this by pointing to the counters that the volunteer student has placed on the demonstration ten-frame. Call out the amount and have the volunteer record that number in the first blank on his sheet. Next, ask the class how many squares do not have counters and ask the volunteer to record that number. Finally, have the class work together to find the sum. Have the volunteer record the sum on his sheet. For example, if the ten-frame has four counters on it, the first number sentence would look like this:

$$4 + 6 = 10$$

Using Spinners Instead of Dice

In Part 2 the dice are replaced by a spinner. Using a 1–10 spinner instead of dice alleviates the additional step of having to figure out the sum of the dice. Instead, students focus on figuring out the sum on their recording sheets and looking for the combinations of ten on the ten-frame.

4. Repeat the steps of play, only this time have the volunteer student pass the spinner to you. Spin it and call out the number. Ask the students if the ten-frame needs "more or less" counters to match the number on the spinner. When they have told you, move the counters on the demonstration ten-frame accordingly and focus students' attention on your own recording sheet. Ask them, "How many squares on the ten-frame have counters?" Then ask, "How many squares do not have counters?" Finally, have the class work to find the sum, and record the number sentence on your recording sheet.

5. Use the game directions to further model the game with students. Make sure to ask students if they have any questions before turning the game over to them.

6. Pass out one ten-frame, one spinner, ten counters, and two copies of the *More or Less* recording sheet to each pair of students.

7. As students play the game, circulate and ask questions. In addition to the key questions, consider these questions:

   ▶ What number sentence matches what you see on your ten-frame?

   ▶ What do all your number sentences have in common? (the sum of ten)

Differentiating Your Instruction

Additional Support
If students need more modeling and support in using the recording sheet, consider having the class play Part 1 of this game while you work with a few students at a time to introduce Part 2.

Teaching Tip

Asking Key Questions
The purpose of using key questions during game play is to engage students in conversations about mathematical ideas. The purpose is not to ask all students all key questions. Choose a few key questions to ask students as you move from group to group. These conversations allow you to informally assess what students know and advance students' thinking to a new level. Listening to students' answers can inform the instructional choices you make as a teacher. For instance, if you notice several students are struggling to add the numbers, consider carving out time to work on fact practice.

More or Less, Part 2

Objective

Players use a spinner, a ten-frame and counters, and a recording sheet to create and record combinations of ten.

Materials

1 ten-frame, 1 spinner, 10 counters, and 2 copies of the *More or Less* recording sheet for each pair of players

Directions

1. Player A spins the spinner and calls out the number it lands on. Player A places that number of counters on the ten-frame.

2. On his or her recording sheet, in the first blank, Player A records the number of squares on the ten-frame that have counters. In the second blank, he or she records the number of squares without counters (empty squares). Thirdly, Player A adds the numbers together and records the sum.

3. Player A passes the spinner to Player B. Player B repeats Steps 1 and 2, this time adding or removing counters on the ten-frame as needed and recording the information on his or her recording sheet.

4. Players continue taking turns until they have both completed their recording sheets.

Homework

For homework, you can send materials and game directions home with a note attached asking the parent and child to play the game one time, to fill a whole recording sheet.

From *It Makes Sense! Using Ten-Frames to Build Number Sense, Grades K–2* by Melissa Conklin. © 2010 by Math Solutions. Permission granted to photocopy for nonprofit use in a classroom or similar place dedicated to face-to-face educational instruction.

Teaching Directions

Part 3: Summarizing the Game

1. Summarize the game either on the day students have played it or later during the week (when they have had ample time to play the game). Remind students that they worked on sums of ten while playing the game and you would like them to think about the combinations of ten they found.

2. Start the discussion by asking students, "Visualize a ten-frame in your mind and pretend that it has eight counters on it." Ask them to think about what number sentence they would record to show the counters, the empty squares, and the sum.

3. Call on a few students to explain their thinking. Write down the number sentence $8 + 2 = 10$ for the class to see.

4. Repeat the questioning, only this time ask students to pretend the ten-frame has "less" counters; the new amount of counters is five. Ask students to think about what number sentence they would record to show the counters, the empty squares, and the sum.

5. Call on a few students to explain their thinking. Write down the number sentence $5 + 5 = 10$ for the class to see.

6. Repeat your questioning using additional examples.

A Child's Mind . . .

The purpose of summarizing the game this way is to build students' understanding of part-whole relationships where one of the parts is unknown. By visualizing the ten-frame, students begin to internalize the ten-frame tool so that it is no longer necessary to physically have it in front of them.

Teacher Reflection

My *More or Less* Experiences

Introducing Part 2 to Small Groups

I asked my class to play Part 1 of the *More or Less* game while I pulled four students to the small-group table to work with them on Part 2. Our focus was on how to use the *More or Less* recording sheet.

"We're going to use a one-to-ten spinner today so we can focus on looking for combinations of ten while we play *More or Less*," I explained. I showed the four students the spinner. I placed a ten-frame and ten counters on the table and spun the spinner. It landed on 7. I asked Maria to place seven counters on the ten-frame.

"How many squares on the ten-frame are filled with cubes?" I asked.

Maria said, "Seven," and I modeled writing *7* on my recording sheet.

"How many squares are empty?" I asked.

Three of the students counted the squares while Maria called out, "Three," and told us she just knew it was three by looking. I modeled writing *3* on the recording sheet.

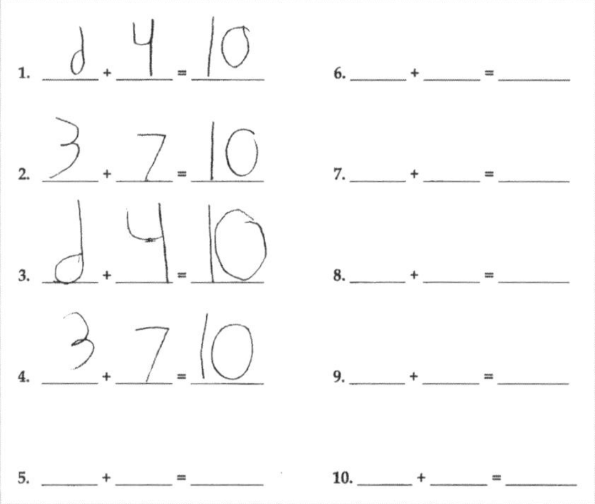

FIGURE G-4.1 As Chris played, he told me he was rolling lots of sixes and threes, and said he would remember six and four was ten, and three and seven was also ten

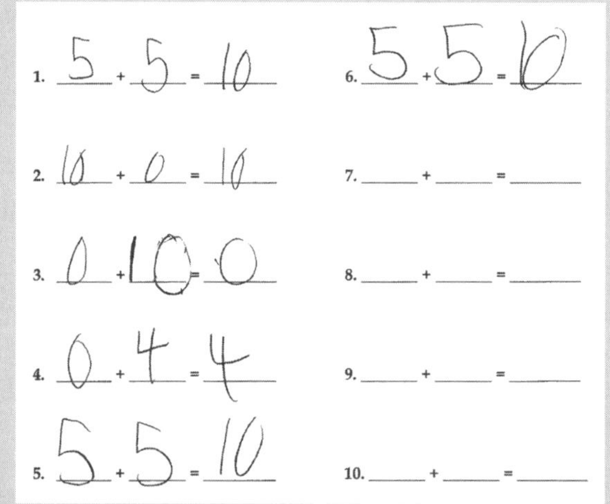

FIGURE G-4.2 Monica enjoyed playing the game but was challenged with writing a number sentence

Next I asked, "How much is seven plus three?" I gave the students time to think, then we discussed the sum and their strategies for finding it. I wrote *10* on my recording sheet.

I passed the spinner to Monica and asked her to spin it and place the corresponding number of counters on the ten-frame. Monica spun a 4, cleared the ten-frame, and put four counters on it.

Maria and Joseph both asked in unison, "Why did you take them all off!?"

I asked Joseph to tell us what he would have done differently. Joseph explained that he would have taken only some of the counters off the ten-frame. To demonstrate, he put seven counters back on the ten-frame and took off one at a time until he had four counters. I commented that there were several ways to build a number and that was certainly one way, as was Monica's way of clearing and rebuilding.

"Monica, how many squares are filled on the ten-frame?" I asked.

Monica said, "Four," and I modeled recording *4* on the recording sheet.

"How many squares are empty?" I asked the group.

After some thinking, they all said, "Six," and I modeled recording *6* on the recording sheet. We discussed how to figure out the sum of 4 + 6 and then I wrote *10* on the recording sheet.

I played several more rounds with this small group of students before giving them their own recording sheet and leaving them to try out the game by themselves. I then proceeded to other groups and introduced Part 2, with the spinner and the recording sheet, when it seemed appropriate.

See Figures G-4.1 and G-4.2 for two students' completed recording sheets.

FIGURE G-4.3 In *More or Less*, Part 1, Keeley rolled a sum of nine and began to build on to Michael's previous round of play

FIGURE G-4.4 In *More or Less*, Part 1, Michael decided to help Keeley put her last cube on the ten-frame

Game 5

Make Five

Overview

In this game, students try to pair up ten-frame cards to get a sum of five. Like ten and one hundred, five is an important landmark number, especially to primary-aged students. As an added bonus, the game requires that students practice other addition facts in their quest for combinations of five. Part 1 allows students to learn and play the game without recording. Part 2 builds upon their understanding by asking them to record their thinking while playing the game. An assessment game, *Secret Number*, gives teachers information about students' progress as they learn their facts.

Related Lessons

Consider these lessons as a follow-up:

▶ G-6 Collect Ten

▶ G-7 Bank It!

Key Questions

▶ What two cards have a sum of five? How do you know?

▶ What card would partner with the cards you see to create a sum of five?

▶ You are about to draw from the deck; what do you hope to draw? Why?

Time

20–30 minutes

Materials

ten-frame cards (Reproducible B), 4 sets per group of 2–4 students

Make Five recording sheet (Reproducible 9), 1 copy for the teacher and 1 copy per student

Teaching Directions

Part 1: Playing *Make Five*

1. Gather four sets of ten-frame cards. Remove the 6–10 ten-frame cards and place them somewhere where they won't be used or get confused with the 1–5 ten-frame cards. The four sets of 1–5 cards constitute a deck for this game.

2. Explain to students that they will be playing a game using a partial deck of 1–5 ten-frame cards. Shuffle your deck of 1–5 ten-frame cards. Place the shuffled cards facedown and explain that this is called the deck.

3. Ask a student volunteer to help you model the game for the class. Tell the volunteer, "Turn five cards over from the top of the deck. Place the cards faceup and in a straight line." Ask the class to think quietly to determine if there are two cards in the line that equal a sum of five. Have students turn to their partners and discuss.

4. Ask the volunteer, "Do you see two cards with a sum of five?"

    ▶ If the volunteer does, ask him to pick up the two cards and place them next to him. Then instruct the volunteer to re-place the two cards in the line with two more cards from the deck.

    ▶ If there are not two cards in the line that have a sum of five, ask the volunteer to draw one card from the deck and place it on top of one of the five cards in the line.

    ▶ If one of the cards has five dots, ask the volunteer to pick it up and place it next to him. Then instruct the volunteer to replace it with another card from the deck.

5. Let the volunteer know that his turn is over and it is now your turn. Emphasize to students that they need to make sure, at the end of every turn, that there are only five cards faceup.

Teaching Tip

Shuffling Cards
To model a child-friendly way of shuffling cards, place the cards facedown on a table and move them around with both hands until they are mixed up. Then stack them randomly together.

Teaching Tip

Modeling a Game
Have students sit in a circle in the whole-group area and place the cards in the middle of the circle so every child can see. Alternatively, have the students sit in the whole-group area and place the cards in a pocket chart.

Teaching Tip

Supporting ELLs
If necessary, or to support English language learners, introduce the word *sum* by writing it for the class to see, reading the word, and defining it for students: "When we put two amounts together, we call that number the sum." Write a number sentence such as *3 + 2 = 5* and write *sum* under the 5. Consider introducing *addend* to students by telling them mathematicians call the 3 and 2 addends and writing *addends* under the 3 and 2. (See *Supporting English Language Learners in Math Class, Grades K–2* by Rusty Bresser, Kathy Melanese, and Christine Sphar, © 2009 Math Solutions.)

6. In modeling your turn, point to one of the five cards in the line and ask students, "What card can be paired with this card to create a sum of five?" Give students time to think and discuss with partners. Do this with each faceup card. Your next step will then be one of the following:

   ▶ If there are two cards in the line with a sum of five, remove them from the line and place them next to you. Before replacing the two cards in the line with two more cards from the deck (there should be always five cards in the line), ask students, "I am about to draw from the deck; what do you hope I draw? Why?" Have students discuss their thinking with their partners, then share their answers with the class.

   ▶ If there are not two cards in the line that have a sum of five, draw one card from the deck and place it on top of one of the five cards in the line.

   ▶ Let students know that your turn is over.

7. Use the game directions to further model the game until all the cards have been used. Make sure to ask students if they have any questions before turning the game over to them.

8. Have students play the game in small groups of two to four players. Pass out four sets of ten-frame cards to each group and instruct the students on how to create a deck for playing this game.

9. As students play the game, circulate and ask questions (refer to the key questions).

Differentiating Your Instruction

Playing the Game Individually

Though the steps indicate that students should play this game in groups of two to four, it can also be played individually. Consider having a student play individually if he or she is struggling to work with others that day, finishes work before the rest of the class, or arrives early to school.

Make Five

Objective

Players work through a deck of 1–5 ten-frame cards, trying to make pairs of cards that have a sum of five. Although the winner is the person who has the most cards, emphasize that the goal is for students to play until no cards remain.

Materials

4 sets of ten-frame cards for each group of 2–4 players

Directions

1. Remove the cards 6–10 from your four sets of ten-frame cards and place them somewhere safe where they won't be used or get confused with the 1–5 ten-frame cards. Shuffle the four sets of 1–5 ten-frame cards together. Place the shuffled cards facedown to form a deck. Turn five cards over from the top of the deck. Place the cards faceup and in a straight line.

2. Player A studies the line of cards to determine if there are two cards with a sum of five:

    ▶ If there are two cards with a sum of five, Player A picks up the two cards and places them to the side. Then he or she replaces the two cards in the line with two more cards from the deck (there should be always five cards in the line). Player A's turn is now over.

    ▶ If there are not two cards with a sum of five, Player A draws one card from the deck and places it on top of one of the five cards in the line. Player A's turn is now over.

3. Player B studies the new line of cards to determine if there are two cards with a sum of five, then follows Step 2 above.

4. All players follow the same procedure until all the cards in the deck have been paired. The winner is the person with the most cards.

Teaching Tip

The 5 Card

When a 5 card comes up, the player whose turn it is should pick it up, place it with his or her pile of cards, and allow the other player to take a turn. The point of including the 5 card in the deck of playing cards is to give students opportunities to subitize five—that is, see the amount of five. Subitizing is important as students develop counting-on strategies. When students subitize, they understand that they are looking at a collection of objects and do not need to begin counting from one.

Homework

For homework, you can send materials and game directions home with a note attached asking the parent and child to play the game three times or asking the parent to monitor as the child plays the game three times by himself or herself.

Teaching Tip

Recording the 5 Card

When students are playing *Make Five* using the recording sheet, and the 5 card comes up, they need to pick the card up from the line and record either *5 + 0 = 5* or *5 = 5* on their recording sheets.

Differentiating Your Instruction

Recording

Some students may be ready to record the combinations of five and some may need more time to become comfortable with the game. Allow students to begin recording when they are ready to.

Teaching Directions

Part 2: Using the Recording Sheet

1. On another day, after students are familiar and comfortable with playing *Make Five*, explain to them that they are now going to record the combinations of five they make with their cards.

2. Ask a volunteer student to help you model the game using the *Make Five* recording sheet (Reproducible 9). When there are two cards with a sum of five, have the volunteer write the number of the first card in the first blank on her recording sheet, then write the number of the second card in the second blank. Finally, the volunteer should fill in the sum (which should always be five). She should now have a complete number sentence on her recording sheet.

3. Repeat modeling how to use the recording sheet, this time as you take your turn. Find two cards with a sum of five and model holding up one card and writing the number in the first blank on the recording sheet, then write the number of the second card in the second blank. Finally, record the sum. Continue to model for several more rounds.

4. Pass out the materials to students and circulate while they are playing to answer any questions they may have about recording.

Assessment: Make Five

While groups of students are playing *Make Five*, meet with students one-on-one and play *Secret Card* with them. Explain to the student that in the game of *Secret Card*, he'll still be working to make sums of five, but you are going to be hiding a secret card from him. You'll give him a clue by telling him what card should be matched with the secret card to make a sum of five. For example, hide the 2 card. Tell the student that the card that should be matched with the secret card is the 3 card. Ask the student, "What card do I have to match with the three card to make a sum of five?"

To record students' understanding, use the *Secret Card* assessment rubric (Reproducible 10). Teachers can use this rubric to keep track of where each child is in his or her learning journey, as a guide to plan future lessons, or as a reference tool during parent conferences.

Secret Card Assessment Rubric

Secret Number (Ask out of order.)	Knows the Secret Number Instantly	Uses a Counting Strategy to Figure Out the Secret Number and Is Correct	Uses a Counting Strategy to Figure Out the Secret Number and Is Incorrect	Guesses the Secret Number
0				
1				
2				
3				
4				
5				

FIGURE G-5.1 Reproducible 10: *Secret Card* Assessment Rubric

Teacher Reflection

My *Make Five* Experiences

Accommodating All Learning Levels

When I introduce this game to my classes, I move from group to group and pay careful attention to how each student is understanding and playing the game. I am always happy with how this game meets the needs of a wide range of learners. I usually find that some students instantly identify two cards that have a sum of five, while others must count every dot on each ten-frame card in their effort to find two cards with a sum of five.

I frequently engage students in conversation as I circulate. I point to a card and ask how many dots there are on the card, then ask the student to show me how she uses the ten-frame to help her think about how many more dots are needed to have a sum of five. Often students point out that the ten-frame helps in that there are five squares in each row. This helps them create a visual for how many more dots are needed to have a sum of five.

The recording sheet enables students to begin practicing recording their facts and also learn to record during a game. After students use a recording sheet while playing several times, I ask them to record on a blank sheet of paper. The transition from recording sheet to blank paper encourages students to learn and practice writing number sentences.

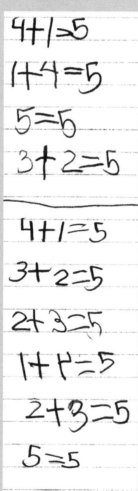

FIGURE G-5.1 Stacey and her partner were able to play two games in the given time

FIGURE G-5.2 Diamond played an individual game of *Make Five* because she had completed her work early

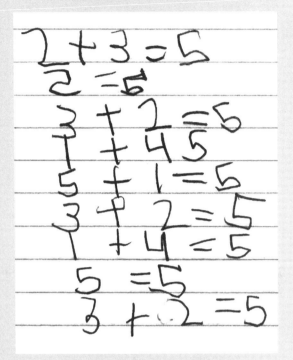

FIGURE G-5.4 Max found several cards with a sum of five

FIGURE G-5.3 While playing with Jenessa, CJ tried to find two cards with a sum of five

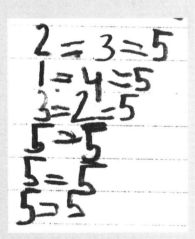

FIGURE G-5.5 Joseph collected pairs with a sum of five and worked on correctly recording number sentences

Game 6

Collect Ten

Overview

In this game, students try to pair up ten-frame cards to get a sum of ten. Ten is a landmark number; by knowing combinations of ten, students can begin to construct relationships when solving other basic facts. Part 1 allows students to learn and play the game without recording. Part 2 builds upon their understanding by asking them to record their thinking while playing the game. A *Collect Ten* assessment gives students experience finding the missing addend in the context of the game.

Related Lessons

You might teach the following lesson first:

▶ G-5 Make Five

Consider this lesson as a follow-up:

▶ G-9 Race to 20

Key Questions

▶ How can you prove _____ and _____ equal ten?

▶ What do you hope to draw? Why?

▶ What are you going to ask for? Why?

Time

20 minutes

Materials

ten-frame cards (Reproducible B), 4 sets per group of 2–4 students

Collect Ten recording sheet (Reproducible 11), 1 copy for the teacher and 1 copy per student

Teaching Directions

Part 1: Playing *Collect Ten*

1. Gather four sets of ten-frame cards. Remove the ten-frame cards with ten dots and place them somewhere where they won't be used or get confused with the remaining ten-frame cards. The four sets of 1–9 cards constitute a deck for this game.

2. Explain to students that they will be playing a game using a partial deck of 1–9 ten-frame cards. Shuffle your deck of 1–9 ten-frame cards. Place the shuffled cards facedown and explain that this is called the deck.

3. Ask a student volunteer to help you model the game for the class. Deal five cards from the shuffled deck to the student. Then give yourself five cards.

4. Spread your cards on the floor so every student can see them (this is for the model game only). Look for pairs of cards that have a sum of ten. Put the pairs aside. Show students how to set each pair aside so that the pairs don't get mixed together; for example, you could place each pair on top of the previous one but perpendicular to it. Ask the student volunteer to spread her cards on the floor for all to see. Ask her to look for pairs of cards that have a sum of ten and to place the pairs aside. (Note: It is possible that a player may still have five cards in hand when the first round is ready to begin.)

5. Ask students, "What card do you think I should ask my partner for so that I can pair it with a card I have to make a sum of ten?" Give them quiet time to think, then ask them to share their thinking with their partners. Ask students to explain their strategies. Decide which card you are going to ask for.

6. Ask the volunteer student if she has the card you want in her hand of cards.

Teaching Tip

Shuffling Cards
To model a child-friendly way of shuffling cards, place the cards facedown on a table and move them around with both hands until they are mixed up. Then stack them randomly together.

Teaching Tip

Supporting ELLs
If necessary, or to support English language learners, introduce the word *sum* by writing it for the class to see, reading the word, and defining it for students: "When we put two amounts together, we call that number the sum." Write a number sentence such as *9 + 1 = 10* and write *sum* under the 10. Consider introducing *addend* to students by telling them mathematicians call the 9 and 1 addends and writing *addends* under the 9 and 1. (See *Supporting English Language Learners in Math Class, Grades K–2* by Rusty Bresser, Kathy Melanese, and Christine Sphar, © 2009 Math Solutions.)

- ▶ If your partner has the card, she must pass it to you. Pair up the card with one of your cards to make the sum of ten and set the pair to the side. Your turn is over.

- ▶ If your partner does not have the card, you must draw one card from the deck. If the card you take from the deck makes a sum of ten with one of your cards, pair them up and place them to the side. If the card you take from the deck does not make a sum of ten with your cards, leave the card in your hand. Your turn is over.

- ▶ If at any point in the game you have no cards left in your hand, but cards are still available in the deck, draw two cards.

7. Tell the volunteer student that it is now her turn.

8. Ask the students what card they think the volunteer student should ask for so that she can pair it with a card she has to make a sum of ten. Give them quiet time to think, then ask them to share their thinking with their partners. Ask students to explain their strategies.

9. Have the volunteer ask you if you have the card she wants.

- ▶ If you have the card, you must pass it to the volunteer. The volunteer pairs up the card with one of her cards to make the sum of ten and sets the pair to the side. Her turn is over.

- ▶ If you do not have the card, the volunteer must draw one card from the deck. If the card she takes from the deck makes a sum of ten with one of her cards, she should pair them up and place them to the side. If the card she takes from the deck does not make a sum of ten with her cards, she should leave the card in her hand. Her turn is over.

▶ If at any point in the game she has no cards left in her hand, but cards are still available in the deck, she should draw two cards.

10. Use the game directions to further model the game. Make sure to ask students if they have any questions before turning the game over to them.

11. Have students play the game in small groups of two to four players. Pass out four sets of cards and remind students to remove the cards with ten dots.

12. As students play the game, circulate and ask questions (refer to the key questions).

Differentiating Your Instruction

Playing the Game Individually

If a student would benefit from playing *Collect Ten* without a partner or small group, refer to the directions for the *Make Five* game (see G-5 in this section of the book). Allow the student to use a deck of ten-frame cards as assembled for *Collect Ten* but follow the playing format of *Make Five*.

Collect Ten

Objective

Players work through a deck of 1–9 ten-frame cards, trying to make pairs of cards that have a sum of ten. The winner is the person with the most cards.

Materials

4 sets of ten-frame cards for each group of 2–4 players

Directions

1. Remove the cards with ten dots from your four sets of ten-frame cards and place them somewhere where they won't be used or get confused with the rest of the cards. Shuffle the remaining cards. Deal five cards out to each player. Place the rest of the shuffled cards facedown to form a deck.

2. Each player looks at his or her hand of five cards. If any player has two cards that make a sum of ten, that player pairs up the cards and places them to the side, being careful not to mix up the pairs. For example, the player can place each pair on top of the previous one but perpendicular to it to keep each pair separate. (Note: It is possible that a player may still have five cards in hand when the first round is ready to begin.)

3. Player A thinks about what card he or she needs to pair up with one of his or her cards to make a sum of ten. Player A then chooses to ask another player for the card.

   ▶ If Player A receives the card, he or she pairs it up to make the sum of ten and sets the pair to the side. Player A's turn is now over.

   ▶ If Player A does not receive the card, he or she must draw one card from the deck. If the card Player A takes from the deck makes a sum of ten with one of the cards in his or her hand, Player A must pair them up and place them aside. Player A's turn is now over. If the card Player A takes from the deck does not make a sum of ten with his or her cards, the card should remain in his or her hand. Players A's turn is over.

   ▶ If at any point in the game a player has no cards left in his or her hand, but cards are still available in the deck, the player should draw two cards.

4. All players follow the same procedure until all the cards in the deck have been paired.

5. Players record their pairs of cards using a recording sheet or a piece of paper. The winner is the person with the most cards.

Homework

For homework, you can send materials and game directions home with a note attached asking the parent and child to play the game three times.

From *It Makes Sense! Using Ten-Frames to Build Number Sense, Grades K–2* by Melissa Conklin. © 2010 by Math Solutions. Permission granted to photocopy for nonprofit use in a classroom or similar place dedicated to face-to-face educational instruction.

Teaching Directions

Part 2: Using the Recording Sheet

1. On another day, after students are familiar and comfortable with playing *Collect Ten*, explain to them that they are now going to record the combinations of ten they make with their cards.

2. Ask a volunteer student to help you model the game using the *Collect Ten* recording sheet (Reproducible 11). When the game is finished, model how to record by picking up two cards that are paired together. Write the first card in the first blank on the recording sheet. Then write the number of the second card in the second blank. Last, fill in the sum—which should always be ten. Ask the volunteer to begin recording as you finish recording all the pairs of cards.

3. Emphasize that it's especially important to keep each pair of cards separate from the other pairs; this will help them see the combinations of ten when the game is over. Explain to them that when they are finished recording they will figure out the total amount of points they have earned by adding up all the tens and completing the last part of their recording sheets. Finally, each student will compare his point total to his partner's point total (or the total of another player in the group).

4. Pass out one copy of the *Collect Ten* recording sheet to each student. Make sure students still have their sets of ten-frame cards. As students play the game using their recording sheets, circulate and ask questions (refer to the key questions).

5. When students are finished playing the game, and before having them clean up the materials, ask them to check their recording sheets and remember two combinations of ten that they found.

Differentiating Your Instruction

Using Actual Playing Cards
When you notice students becoming more familiar with the facts for ten and you feel they're ready for a more challenging game, swap out their decks of ten-frame cards with actual playing cards. Remove the 10 and face cards from the deck. Because students no longer have the ten-frame on each card as support, they must now rely on other strategies to know what to ask for to make a sum of ten. On the other hand, if *Collect Ten* is too challenging for a student, have her try the *Make Five* game (see G-5 in this section of the book).

Teaching Tip

Managing Your Classroom
By asking students to remember two combinations of ten, you'll alleviate the problems that bringing recording sheets to the whole-group area can create. If, on the other hand, you decide to have students bring their recording sheets to the whole-group area, set expectations for what students should do with their recording sheets during the discussion (they should place the sheets in front of them and refrain from playing with them).

6. Gather the class together for a whole-group discussion on combinations of ten. Ask students to tell you what combinations of ten they remember finding in the game. Record students' answers so eventually you have a list in order like the following:

$1 + 9 = 10$

$2 + 8 = 10$

$3 + 7 = 10$

$4 + 6 = 10$

$5 + 5 = 10$

$6 + 4 = 10$

$7 + 3 = 10$

$8 + 2 = 10$

$9 + 1 = 10$

Ask students to discuss what they notice about the list.

Assessment: Collect Ten

After students have had repeated experiences playing *Collect Ten*, use the *Collect Ten* assessment (Reproducible 12) to assess their thinking. Teachers can use this assessment in small groups to clarify any confusion students may have about the questions, or during whole group as a traditional quiz or test.

Finding the missing addend can be a difficult but important skill for students; using a context they are familiar with helps them think more about the missing addend. In addition, the last question of the assessment allows students to think more about the game than just "that was fun." and to communicate what they learned from the game.

Teachers can use this assessment to keep track of where each child is in his or her learning journey, to explore concepts and skills that may arise unexpectedly from the assessment, and as a guide to plan future lessons or class discussion.

Teacher Reflection

My *Collect Ten* Experiences
Introducing the Game

As my students came in from lunch one day, I asked them to sit in a circle on the rug. My students routinely gather on the rug during the introduction of math lessons. I told them that during math today their focus would be on learning their combinations of ten; we were going to play a game to help them. I introduced the game *Collect Ten* by displaying the game directions in front of the class.

"Today, you'll work to collect two cards that have a sum of ten," I told the class.

"What does *sum* mean?" Vincent wondered aloud.

"*Sum* is the total amount when you combine two or more numbers," I explained. I wrote the word *sum* on the board. Next to the word, I wrote the definition *total amount*. I knew some kids, especially second language learners, might think I was saying *son* or *some*. I wanted to give them a visual reference to the new vocabulary word. I also wrote the following on the board and explained the nine and one were called addends and the ten was the sum.

$$9 + 1 = 10 \ (sum)$$

$$9$$

$$\underline{+\ 1}$$

$$10 \ (sum)$$

I then proceeded with the game directions. "To play *Collect Ten*, you will first need four sets of ten-frame cards. Remove all of the cards with ten dots and set them aside, mix up or shuffle the rest of your cards, and pass five cards out to your friend and five cards to yourself." I choose Malcolm as my partner.

I shuffled the ten-frame cards (after removing the 10 cards) and dealt five cards to Malcolm. I then kept five for myself. I put the remaining cards into a pile and explained to the students that this was the deck from which they would be drawing cards.

I spread my five cards out so that everyone could see them. I asked students to find any pairs with a sum of ten. I reminded them to think quietly, then I asked them to share their thinking with their partners. I gave students time to discuss, then I called on Sergio.

"Sergio, tell me a pair of cards that you found."

Sergio grinned and exclaimed, "Nine and one make ten!"

I made sure the rest of the class was thinking about what Sergio said. "Sergio thinks the sum of nine and one is ten. Do you agree with Sergio? How can you prove that?"

Farrah eagerly shared, "There's one empty space on the nine card, so you know you just need one more to fill up the card and then you have ten!"

Garrett wiggled his thumb and chimed in, "Yeah, and when I put up nine fingers, my thumb is left, and I know I have ten fingers."

"OK," I said, gathering everyone's attention to the cards again. "So I'm going to take the nine and one cards and lay them next to me."

Now it was Malcolm's turn. I asked Malcolm to look for combinations of ten in the five cards he was holding. I explained to students, "Now, the job is to ask the other player for a card that will give you a sum of ten when you combine it with a card that is in your hand." I laid my cards down again for all students to see. "When you look at my cards, what do you think I should ask Malcolm for so that I can collect ten?"

I continued by thinking aloud. "I see I have an eight and I would need two more to make a ten. I know that because I see two empty squares on the ten-frame card marked eight. So I could ask Malcolm for a two. What else might I ask Malcolm for?"

"You could ask him for a three because seven and three make ten," Sydney volunteered.

"How do you know that seven and three make ten?" I asked.

"Well, I saw the seven card and put up seven fingers and three of my fingers were down."

"Thanks for explaining, Sydney. What else might I ask for?"

"A four . . . ," Jose whispered.

"If I ask for a four, what card should I pair it with to make a ten?" I pressed Jose further. Jose tended to be quiet during math class, so I was excited that he spoke, but I also wanted to make sure he knew that the 4 went with the 6 instead of just assuming that's what he was thinking.

Jose timidly continued. "You could put it with the six because there's four empty boxes on the six card."

"So, Jose, Sydney, and I have some suggestions of what I could ask for. I'll use Jose's idea and ask Malcolm if he has a four." I modeled asking Malcolm for a 4, which he had and passed to me. I laid down the 6 and 4 cards and emphasized to students to keep each pair of cards separate from the other pairs. I explained that this would help them see the combinations of ten when the game was over. We continued playing the game, stopping often to discuss what I might ask for or what I was hoping to draw from the deck.

Using the Recording Sheet

On the second day of playing *Collect Ten*, I played another whole-class game with my students. This time my purpose was to introduce the *Collect Ten* recording sheet. My partner and I played the game as we did the day before until all the cards in the draw pile and our hands were gone. I then took the cards I'd collected and modeled how to write my equations on the *Collect Ten* recording sheet.

"The recording sheet asks us to figure out our points for the game. The points are the sum of all your cards. Since we grouped them by tens, we can count by tens to help us," I explained to the class. As we counted, I move each pair of cards that equaled ten to the side until we had counted all my pairs. I then asked Malcolm to complete his *Collect Ten* recording sheet and figure out his total points for the game.

It was now time for Malcolm and me to compare our totals. I wrote the following sentence prompts on the board so students could refer to them when Malcolm and I did our comparisons; I filled in my total points and Malcolm's total points, so the only blank left to complete was the comparison.

My total for *Collect Ten* is _____.

My total of _____ is _____ than my partner's total of _____.

I reminded the class, "When you finish playing, I want you to use these sentences to help you compare your points with your partner's points. I had one hundred points and Malcolm had one hundred and twenty points. How would I compare my points with Malcolm's points?"

"You lost the game because Malcolm has more points," Sydney declared.

"Yes, I do not have as many points as Malcolm. What sentence would I use to help me compare my points with Malcolm's points?" I pushed students to think beyond winning or losing.

"You could say one hundred is smaller than one hundred and twenty," Farrah suggested. I decided to write *smaller than* next to the prompts.

"How else can I compare my points with Malcolm's points?" I wanted my students to verbalize as many ways as possible to say the same concept. I also wanted them to hear and have opportunities to use mathematical vocabulary such as *less than* and *greater than*.

"One hundred is less than one hundred and twenty," Tia said, so I recorded *less than* on the board next to *smaller than*.

I asked Malcolm to compare his points with mine. He used the phrase *bigger than*, and I recorded that under the *smaller than* and *less than* phrases. I also let the students know they could use the phrase *greater than* and recorded it next to *bigger than*.

It was now time to turn the game over to the students. I paired up students and passed out the ten-frame cards and recording sheets. I reminded them they also needed their pencils. Each pair of students then found a place on the floor to settle in and play.

Summarizing the Game

As a means to summarize this game, I asked my students to review the number sentences on their *Collect Ten* recording sheets and choose two to remember so we could begin a class discussion. I then told students to put their *Collect Ten* recording sheets and ten-frame cards on the materials table and take a seat on the floor in the whole-group area.

"I want you to think about the game *Collect Ten* and be ready to tell me a pair of cards you collected that had a sum of ten." I wrote *Collect Ten* at the top of a piece of chart paper. I called on Pablo to tell me a pair he collected.

"I had a lot of eight and two cards," Pablo said. I recorded $8 + 2 = 10$ near the bottom of my chart paper. I thanked him for sharing and then called on Maria.

"I think I had five and five," Maria said, demonstrating with her hands. I recorded $5 + 5 = 10$ near the middle of the chart paper.

"What card could I pair with a nine card to make ten?" I asked, wanting them to think about the missing addend. Several students began using their fingers, several appeared to be visualizing the ten-frame, and some immediately raised their hands.

"One!" Malcolm excitedly answered after I called on him.

"How did you know that one plus nine equals ten?" I asked.

Malcolm defended his answer. "The nine card has one missing spot on it."

I added on to Malcolm's comment by explaining to the class, "Putting a picture of the cards in your head could be helpful to figure out how to make ten." I wrote *9 + 1 = 10* under *8 + 2 = 10*. I called on a few more students until finally our chart looked like this:

Collect Ten

1 + 9 = 10

2 + 8 = 10

4 + 6 = 10

5 + 5 = 10

7 + 3 = 10

8 + 2 = 10

9 + 1 = 10

FIGURE G-6.1 In *Collect Ten*, Part 1, Angel and Zachary looked for two cards with sum of ten in their own hands before beginning the game

FIGURE G-6.2 In *Collect Ten*, Part 1, Viridiana found two cards with a sum of ten

"What do you notice about how I wrote our number sentences so far?" I asked the class. We had studied patterns earlier in the year, so I expected some students to recognize the order of the addends as a pattern. I gave students time to think quietly before asking them to share their thinking with their partners. I reminded them to share their thinking but to also be good listeners. Once I'd given students time to share with their partners, I brought everyone's attention to the chart again.

Nyla was one of the first to volunteer her thoughts. "I see a pattern! It goes up seven, eight, nine."

FIGURE G-6.3 In *Collect Ten*, Part 1, Lionel passed Reese the 7 card she asked for so she could pair it with the 3 card in her hand

"Yeah, and before that there's a one and two, but the three is missing. Then it goes four, five, and the six is missing," Oscar added.

"What else do you notice?" I asked.

"They all equal ten! See, ten, ten, ten, ten, ten," Sydney said, running her finger down the chart, calling off the sums.

"And the other side goes down," Mark affirmed.

"So if we see that one side is counting up and the other side is counting down, how can that help us figure out what is missing?" I gave students some time to think before calling on Kylie.

"See under the one, two we need a three, and then under the nine, eight we need a seven. So write three plus seven," Kylie explained.

"Does three plus seven equal ten? Before you use your fingers, can you put a picture in your mind of the seven card? What do you see when you think about the seven card?"

"Five are filled in and then two more are filled in," Malcolm contributed.

"Yes, on a seven card one row of five is filled in and two more on the other row are filled in. So when you think about a seven card, what is not filled in?" I urged students to think.

"Three!" several students exclaimed in unison.

"Yeah, and that's how you know that seven plus three makes ten!" Tia piped in.

I wrote *7 + 3 = 10* on the chart and told everyone to turn to a partner and discuss what was missing and how he or she knew. I listened in on a few partners before calling on Sergio.

"You need to put six plus four equals ten," Sergio said.

"How do you know the sum of six and four is ten?"

"I saw a picture of the six card in my brain and four is missing, so six and four is ten."

When students use a tool like the ten-frame, they begin to visualize the tool in their minds, as Sergio was doing.

Last but not least, Sydney said, "I think six and four is ten because our chart is a pattern and they all equal ten. You just look at counting on the chart and six comes next, then four, and they all equal ten." Sydney pointed to the chart the entire time she was talking.

I chose to close the discussion at that point. "Those sound like two nice ways to think about how we know six and four is ten. Now we're going to play *Collect Ten* several more times to help us learn our combinations of ten."

Collect Ten Assessment

1. I was playing *Collect Ten* with a friend. My hand looked like this:

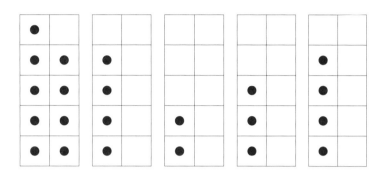

What card should I ask my friend for? Why?

1 Bc us 9+1=10

2. Look at my cards from Question 1. What card should I ask for on my next turn? Why?

6 Bcus 4+6=10

3. My friend asked me for an 8. What card do you think she will match it with to make a sum of 10? How do you know? Use words, numbers, or pictures to explain your thinking.

I now is nes two more

8 9 10

FIGURE G-6.4 On her *Collect Ten* Assessment form, Mikaela recorded how she counted on to solve the third problem

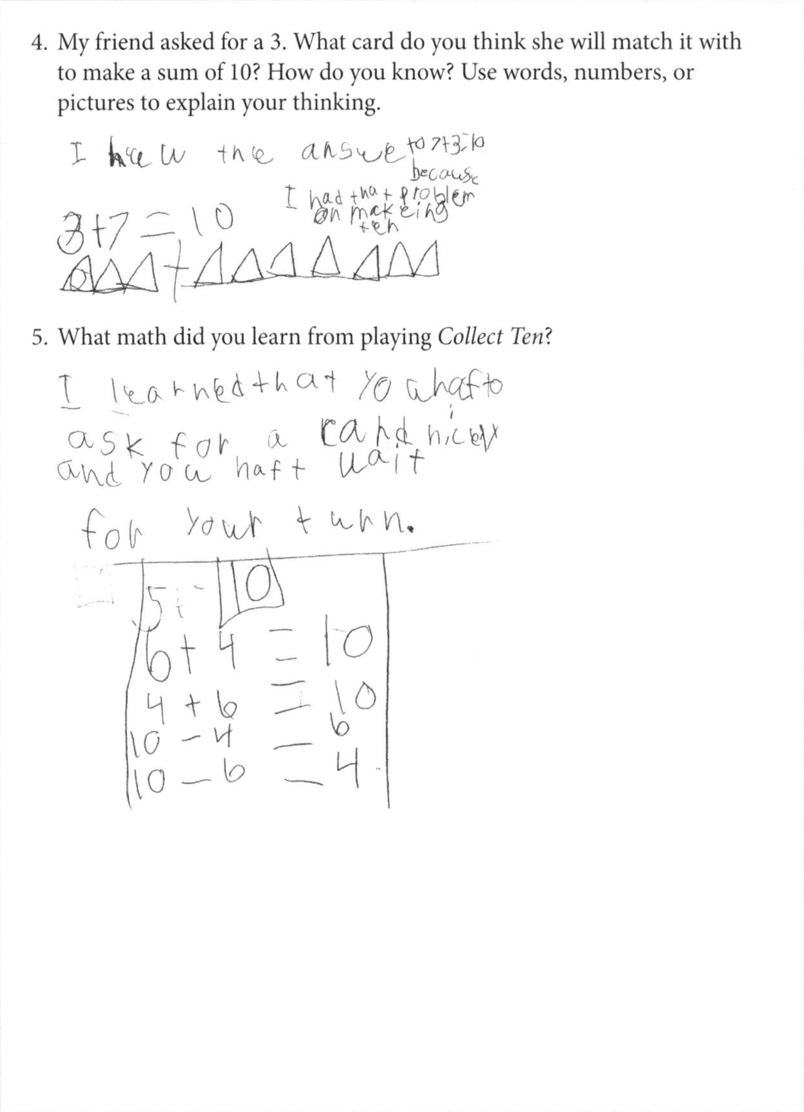

4. My friend asked for a 3. What card do you think she will match it with to make a sum of 10? How do you know? Use words, numbers, or pictures to explain your thinking.

I haew the answer to 7+3=10 because I had that problem on makeing ten

3+7 = 10

△△△ + △△△△△△△

5. What math did you learn from playing *Collect Ten*?

I learned that yo ahafto ask for a cahd nicely and you haft wait for your turn.

5 = 10
6 + 4 = 10
4 + 6 = 10
10 − 4 = 6
10 − 6 = 4

FIGURE G-6.5 On his *Collect Ten* Assessment form, Zachary remembered from playing the game that 3 + 7 = 10; for question 5 he proved to me that students learn more than math while playing games. He finished early and asked if he could record a fact family that equaled ten

Bank It!

Overview

In this game, each student turns over a ten-frame card and compares the number of dots with the dots on his or her partner's card. Being able to compare numbers is an important aspect of number sense. Students intuitively know that some numbers are bigger or smaller than other numbers, but they may not have developed the mathematical vocabulary necessary to express this idea. This game connects common language with mathematical language for comparing numbers. Part 1 focuses on having students orally practice comparing the numbers. Part 2 builds upon their understanding by asking them to record their thinking while playing the game. In addition, students learn the symbols connected to the comparison words and practice choosing which written words and symbols to use when comparing the numbers. Teachers should use this assessment after students have played several rounds of *Bank It!*, used the recording sheet, and taken part in whole-class discussions about the game.

Related Lesson

Consider this lesson as a follow-up:

▸ G-8 Double Bank It!

Key Questions

▸ You turned over a _____ and your partner turned over a _____. What do you wish your partner had turned over?

▸ Who has the greater number? How do you know?

▸ Which sentence frame will you use to compare your cards?

Time

20 minutes

Materials

ten-frame cards (Reproducible B), 4 sets per pair of students

Bank It! recording sheet (Reproducible 13), 1 copy for the teacher and 1 copy per student

Teaching Tip

Choosing Among Vocabulary Words

When modeling *Bank It!*, use the new math vocabulary word (*less than, greater than*) and then restate the question with the more familiar, everyday usage of the word (*smaller than, bigger than*). In this way, students hear mathematical vocabulary along with words they already understand. The use of both allows all students to follow along with the discussion.

Teaching Tip

Shuffling Cards

To model a child-friendly way of shuffling cards, place the cards facedown on a table and move them around with both hands until they are mixed up. Then stack them randomly together.

Teaching Directions

Part 1: Playing *Bank It!*

1. Introduce the game *Bank It!* by discussing the meaning of the word *bank* with students. *Bank* has several definitions, for example:

   ◗ a place where people put money,

   ◗ the side of a river, or

   ◗ storing important items for later use.

2. Explain to students that in the game *Bank It!* they'll have the opportunity to bank cards—meaning they'll store the cards for later—when they get the highest card. The player with the most cards at the end of the game will be considered the winner.

3. Gather four sets of ten-frame cards and shuffle them together. Explain to students that these four complete sets of cards constitute a deck for this game. Ask a student volunteer to help you model the game for the class. Place the shuffled cards facedown. Deal all the cards between the volunteer and you, leaving them facedown. You should each have a stack of twenty cards.

4. Tell students, "Let's count to three. On the count of three, we will each turn over the top card on our stacks." Have students whisper, "One, two, three!"

5. Ask students, "Look at the ten-frame card we each turned over. Tell a partner how many dots you see." Ask a few volunteers to explain how they knew how many dots were on each card.

6. Now ask students, "Whose card has more dots?" Call on a few volunteers to describe their thinking. Students may say, for example, when comparing three and eight, "I can see that there are more dots on the card," "When I count I say three first," and "I looked at the calendar and eight is after three."

7. Tell students that you are now going to compare the two cards. Emphasize that you are going to start with your card.

8. Introduce the following sentence frames to help students compare:

   Sentence Frames for Comparing Cards

   _____ (number) is less than _____ (number).

   _____ (number) is greater than _____ (number).

   _____ (number) is equal to _____ (number).

   Ask students to read the sentence frames with you. Then ask them to think about the word *less* and give other examples of that word. List the examples to the side of or under the "less than" sentence frame. Repeat for the "greater than" and "equal to" sentence frames. For example:

   1. _____ (number) is less than _____ (number). *smaller than, not as much as, fewer than*
   2. _____ (number) is greater than _____ (number). *more than, bigger than, larger than*
   3. _____ (number) is equal to _____ (number). *is the same as, matches*

9. Model comparing your card with the volunteer's card.

10. Have the volunteer compare his card with your card.

11. Ask, "Whose card has the greater number?" The person with the highest card gets to *bank* the two cards—store them for later. The player with the most cards at the end of the game will be considered the winner.

A Child's Mind . . .

Most children compare numbers by stating the larger number first. Specifying that both students must compare the cards ensures that one player will be using phrases like *fewer than* or *less than* on every round.

Teaching Tip

Supporting ELLS
Sentence frames help ELLs use mathematical language in grammatically correct and complete sentences. During a game, sentence frames also help students focus on the mathematics of the game. It is important to introduce sentence frames and how students might complete or correctly use them. (See *Supporting English Language Learners in Math Class, Grades K–2* by Rusty Bresser, Kathy Melanese, and Christine Sphar, © 2009 Math Solutions.)

A Child's Mind . . .

Some children will be surprised to discover that they are always saying the opposite of what their partner says, except in cases where both cards are the same. Ask students to explain why this is the case.

Differentiating Your Instruction

Additional Support

Work with students who are having trouble using the sentence frames. You can have students repeat the comparisons after you. Also, consider changing the prompts to use *smaller* instead of *less* or *bigger* instead of *greater*.

12. Use the game directions to further model the game. Make sure to discuss what to do if players turn over the same card. In this case, each player should leave the card there, turn over another card, and place it on top of the previously played card. Players should compare the cards; the person with the higher card takes all four cards. Ask students if they have any questions before turning the game over to them.

13. Have students play the game in pairs. Pass out four sets of ten-frame cards to each pair. Emphasize that as students play the game, they should focus on using the sentence frames when comparing their cards (at least until they are using the prompts on their own).

14. As students play the game, circulate and ask questions (refer to the key questions).

Bank It!

Objective

Each player turns over one ten-frame card and compares the number of dots with those on his or her partner's card. The player with the greater card banks both cards. The player with the most banked cards at the end of the game is the winner.

Materials

4 sets of ten-frame cards for each pair of players

Directions

1. Shuffle your four sets of ten-frame cards together. Place the cards facedown. Deal all the cards, leaving them facedown. Each of the two players should have a stack of twenty cards.

2. Players count to three and turn over the top card in each stack.

3. Beginning with Player A, each player compares his or her card with his or her partner's card. Use these sentence frames to help:

Sentence Frames for Comparing Cards

1. _____ (number) is less than _____ (number).
2. _____ (number) is greater than (number).
3. _____ (number) is equal to _____ (number).

4. Whose card has the greater number? The player with the highest card gets to *bank* the cards (store them for later).

5. Repeat Steps 2–4 until all the cards have been banked.

6. If players turn over the same cards, players should draw again and compare the new cards. The player with the greater number should *bank* all four cards.

7. The player with the most cards at the end of the game is the winner.

Alternative

Play again; this time the player with the *smaller* card banks both cards.

Homework

For homework, you can send materials and game directions home with a note attached asking the parent and child to play the game three times.

Differentiating Your Instruction

Making the Most of the Recording Sheet
Copy the *Bank It!* recording sheet on both sides of the paper so that when partners finish before other groups, they can play another game by turning their sheets over.

Students who are familiar with *Bank It!* can record their games in their math journals or on scratch paper using the format of the recording sheet. Using their own paper means they will be responsible for writing in the comparison symbols and words; make sure the sentence frames and symbols are displayed such that all students can see and use them for support.

Teaching Directions

Part 2: Using the Recording Sheet

1. On another day, when students are familiar and comfortable with playing *Bank It!*, explain to them that they are now going to record their comparisons.

2. Bring students' attention to the sentence frames. Introduce the symbols for *less than*, *greater than*, and *equal to*. Tell students, "Mathematicians write these symbols when they compare numbers." Write the corresponding symbol next to each sentence frame:

Sentence Frames for Comparing Cards

1. _____ (number) is less than _____ (number). *smaller than, not as much as, fewer than, <*
2. _____ (number) is greater than _____ (number). *more than, bigger than, larger than, >*
3. _____ (number) is equal to _____ (number). *is the same as, matches, =*

3. Write a comparison equation, such as $7 > 2$, and show students how to find the words that match the symbol. Point to the > sign and then to the words it represents. Read the comparison equation to the class, "Seven is greater than two."

4. Write another comparison equation, such as $5 < 9$. Ask students to look for the symbol in the list of sentence frames and find the words it represents. Ask them to turn to their partners and compare the numbers using the words:

"Five is less than nine."

"Five is smaller than nine."

"Five is not as much as nine."

5. Introduce the *Bank It!* recording sheet (Reproducible 13). Ask a volunteer student to help you model the game using the recording sheet. You should each have a copy of the recording sheet.

6. Write your name on the left-hand side of your recording sheet. Ask the volunteer to write her name on the right-hand side of your recording sheet.

   Then, ask the volunteer to write her name on the left-hand side of her recording sheet and write your name on the right-hand side. Emphasize the importance of writing your names down in the right places!

7. Play one round of *Bank It!* Record the numbers from the cards in the first two blanks of your recording sheet, pointing out to students that you are recording your card's number in the first blank.

8. Ask students, "Look at the sentence frames. Which symbol and words should I circle to correctly compare the numbers?" Give them quiet time to think, then ask them to share their thinking with their partners.

9. Ask students to share which symbol and words you should circle. Make sure they explain their thinking. Circle their choice on your recording sheet. Have the class practice comparing the numbers by reading the comparison out loud.

10. Now it's the volunteer student's turn. Have the volunteer record the numbers from the cards on her recording sheet, this time recording her card's number in the first blank, followed by your card's number.

11. Ask students, "Look at the sentence frames. Which symbol and words should be circled to correctly compare the numbers?" Give them quiet time to think, then ask them to share their thinking with their partners.

12. Ask the volunteer to tell the class which one she thinks should be circled. Have her circle it on her recording sheet. Have the class practice comparing the numbers by reading the comparison out loud.

13. Repeat modeling how to use the recording sheet until students are comfortable with using it. Make sure to ask students if they have any questions.

14. Pass out one copy of the *Bank It!* recording sheet to each student. Make sure students still have their sets of ten-frame cards. As students play the game using their recording sheets, circulate and ask questions (refer to the key questions).

Part 3: Summarizing the Game

1. On another day, after students have played several rounds using the recording sheet, begin a whole-class discussion about the game.

2. Write *8 is greater than (>)* _____ where all students can see it. Ask students, "What number could make this comparison statement true?" Give them quiet time to think, then ask them to each show the number they are thinking of with their fingers.

3. Tell students, "Look around at your classmates. What numbers do you see on their fingers?" Call on a student to read the comparison statement using the number she is showing. Record it under the original comparison statement, this time using just the > symbol:

    8 is greater than (>) _____

    8 > 6

4. Continue calling on students and recording their thinking.

5. Introduce a new equation. Write _____ *is greater than (>) 3* where all students can see it. Ask students, "What number could make this comparison statement true?" Give them quiet time to think, then ask them to share their thinking with their partners.

6. Call on a student to read the comparison statement using his number. Record it under the original comparison statement, this time using just the > symbol:

    _____ *is greater than (>) 3*

    10 > 3

7. Repeat your questioning using additional examples.

Assessment: Bank It!

After students have had repeated experiences playing *Bank It!,* use the *Bank It!* assessment (Reproducible 14) to assess their thinking in small groups or during whole group. During this assessment, students record symbols, words, and a number to correctly complete a comparison statement and also have the opportunity to explain how they know which comparison symbol and words to use. If you choose to have students explain their thinking, it is important to encourage and demonstrate this skill during class discussions prior to the assessment.

Bank It! Assessment

Directions

Fill in the following with one of the comparison symbols and explain your thinking below.

< (is less than)   > (is greater than)   = (is equal to)

1. 9   6
2. 5   8
3. 1   1
4. 7   5
5. 4   6

Choose one problem. How do you know what symbol to use?

Directions

Fill in the following with a number that makes the comparison true and explain your thinking below.

< (is less than)   > (is greater than)   = (is equal to)

6. 8   > (is greater than)   ____
7. 6   < (is less than)   ____
8. 3   < (is less than)   ____
9. 2   > (is greater than)   ____
10. 7   = (is equal to)   ____

Choose one problem. How do you know what number to use?

FIGURE G-7.1 Reproducible 14: *Bank It!* Assessment

Game 8

Double Bank It!

Overview

In this game, each student turns over two ten-frame cards, finds the sum of the numbers, and compares the sum of his or her cards with the sum of his or her partner's cards. It's essential that students have opportunities to make comparison statements about two equations. This opportunity gives them another chance to learn the meaning of *greater than* and *less than* while also helping them build an understanding that the equal sign means that the quantities on either side are the same (students often believe that the equal sign means the answer is coming or an action is going to take place). Teachers should use this assessment after students have played several rounds of *Double Bank It!*, used the recording sheet, and taken part in whole-class discussions about the game.

Related Lessons

You might teach the following lesson first:

▶ G-7 Bank It!

Consider these lessons as a follow-up:

▶ P-2 Riddles

▶ P-3 Mystery Sums

Key Questions

▶ What is the sum of your two cards? How did you figure it out?

▶ Which sum is greater? How do you know?

Time

20 minutes

Materials

demonstration ten-frame cards (see Reproducible B), 2 sets

ten-frame cards (Reproducible B), 4 sets per pair of students

Double Bank It! recording sheet (Reproducible 15), 1 copy for the teacher and 1 copy per student

Extension

demonstration ten-frame cards (see Reproducible B), 1 set

Teaching Directions

Part 1: Playing *Double Bank It!*

1. Familiarize yourself with the rules of *Bank It!* (see G-7 in this section of the book). If your students have previously played *Bank It!* ask them what they remember about playing it. If your students have not yet played *Bank It!* introduce *Double Bank It!* by discussing the meaning of the word *bank* with students. *Bank* has several definitions, for example:

   ▶ a place where people put money,

   ▶ the side of a river, or

   ▶ storing important items for later use.

2. Explain to students that in the game *Double Bank It!* they'll have the opportunity to bank cards—meaning they'll store the cards for later—when their two cards equal the greater sum. The player with the most cards at the end of the game will be considered the winner.

3. Gather four sets of ten-frame cards and shuffle them together. Explain to students that these four complete sets of cards constitute a deck for this game. Ask a student volunteer to help you model the game for the class. Place the shuffled cards facedown. Deal all the cards between the volunteer and you, leaving them facedown. You should each have a stack of twenty cards.

4. Tell students, "Let's count to three. On the count of three, we will each turn over the top two cards on our stacks." Have students whisper, "One, two, three!"

5. Ask students, "Look at the two ten-frame cards I turned over. What is the sum of the two numbers?" Give students quiet time to figure out the sum while you write the number sentence where everyone can see it. Ask students

---

Teaching Tip

Shuffling Cards

To model a child-friendly way of shuffling cards, place the cards facedown on a table and move them around with both hands until they are mixed up. Then stack them randomly together.

Teaching Tip

Supporting ELLs

If necessary, or to support English language learners, introduce the word *sum* by writing it for the class to see, reading the word, and defining it for students: "When we put two amounts together, we call that number the sum." Write a number sentence such as *3 + 2 = 5* and write *sum* under the 5. Consider introducing *addend* to students by telling them mathematicians call the 3 and 2 addends and writing *addends* under the 3 and 2. (See *Supporting English Language Learners in Math Class, Grades K–2* by Rusty Bresser, Kathy Melanese, and Christine Sphar, © 2009 Math Solutions.)

to say the sum out loud. Ask a few volunteers to explain how they figured out the sum.

6. Record the sum under the number sentence.

7. Repeat the same procedure with the volunteer's two ten-frame cards. Your recording space may look like this:

Teacher's Hand	Student's Hand
7 + 3	1 + 5
10	6

8. Ask students to figure out who has the greater sum. Call on a few volunteers to describe their thinking.

Examples of Student Thinking

"When I look at the number line [posted in the class], ten comes after six."

"When I count, I say six before ten."

"On the calendar [posted in the class], the sixth day comes first."

9. Introduce (or revisit, in the case of students who have played *Bank It!*) the following sentence frames.

Sentence Frames for Comparing Cards

1. _____ (number or sentence) is less than _____ (number or sentence).
2. _____ (number or sentence) is greater than _____ (number or sentence).
3. _____ (number or sentence) is equal to _____ (number or sentence).

Ask students to read the sentence prompts with you. Then ask them to think about the word *less* and give other examples of that word. List the examples to the side of or under the "less than" sentence frame. Repeat for the "greater than" and "equal to" sentence frames. For example:

Teaching Tip

Sentence Frames

Sentence frames help second-language learners use mathematical language in grammatically correct and complete sentences. During a game, sentence frames also help students focus on the mathematics of the game. It is important to introduce sentence frames and how students might complete or correctly use them. (See *Supporting English Language Learners in Math Class, Grades K–2* by Rusty Bresser, Kathy Melanese, and Christine Sphar, © 2009 Math Solutions.)

Sentence Frames for Comparing Cards

1. _____ (number or sentence) is less than _____ (number or sentence). *smaller than, not as much as, fewer than*
2. _____ (number or sentence) is greater than _____ (number or sentence). *more than, bigger than, larger than*
3. _____ (number or sentence) is equal to _____ (number or sentence). *is the same as, matches*

10. Tell students, "Each player should describe how the cards compare by using the cards he or she is holding first." Let students know that they can compare the sums first if that is more comfortable for them, but you would also like them to compare the number sentences. For example, students may say:

    "Ten is greater than six. Seven plus three is greater than one plus five."

11. Starting with the two cards you turned over, model comparing the sums first, then the number sentences. Then have the volunteer do the same, starting with the two cards she turned over.

12. Ask, "Who has the greater sum?" The person with the greater sum gets to "double bank" all four cards—store them for later. The player with the most cards at the end of the game will be considered the winner.

13. Use the game directions to further model the game. Make sure to discuss what to do if players turn over the same sum. In this case, each player should leave the cards there and turn over two more cards. Players should compare the new sums; the player with the greater sum takes all eight cards. Make sure to ask students if they have any questions before turning the game over to them.

Teaching Tip

Scaffolding

Asking students to compare the sums is similar to the process of the game *Bank It!*—it allows them to compare two numbers instead of two equations. Allowing students to compare the sums and then later the number sentences helps students to transition to comparing just equations.

14. Have students play the game in pairs. Pass out four sets of ten-frame cards to each pair. Emphasize that as students play the game, they should focus on using the prompts when comparing their cards (at least until they are using the prompts on their own).

15. As students play the game, circulate and ask questions (refer to the key questions).

Double Bank It!

Objective

Each player turns over two ten-frame cards, determines the sum, and compares the sum of his or her cards with the sum of his or her partner's cards. The player with the higher sum banks all four cards. The player with the most cards at the end of the game is the winner.

Materials

4 sets of ten-frame cards for each pair of players

Directions

1. Shuffle your four sets of ten-frame cards together. Place the cards facedown. Deal all the cards, leaving them facedown. Each of the two players should have a stack of twenty cards.

2. Players count to three and turn over the two top cards in each stack.

3. Players find the sum of their two cards.

4. Beginning with Player A, each player compares his or her sum with his or her partner's sum. Use these sentence frames to help:

Sentence Frames for Comparing Cards

1. _____ (number or sentence) is less than _____ (number or sentence).
2. _____ (number or sentence) is greater than _____ (number or sentence).
3. _____ (number or sentence) is equal to _____ (number or sentence).

5. Whose sum is greater? The player with the highest sum gets to "double bank" all four cards (store them for later).

6. Repeat Steps 2–5 until all the cards have been banked.

7. If players turn over the same sum, players should leave the cards there and turn over two more cards. The player with the greater sum takes all eight cards.

8. The player with the most cards at the end of the game is the winner.

Alternative

Play again; this time the player with the *smaller* sum double banks the cards.

Homework

For homework, you can send materials and game directions home with a note attached asking the parent and child to play the game three times.

Teaching Tip

Having Whole-Class Discussions
Whole-class discussions about a game do not always have to happen at the end of class. Rather, conduct them when all students have experienced the game multiple times.

Teaching Directions

Part 2: Whole-Class Discussion

1. After students have played several rounds, begin a whole-class discussion about the game.

2. Display two pairs of ten-frame cards:

   Pair 1: two cards with one dot each

   Pair 2: two cards with nine dots each

   Ask students, "Which sum is larger?" Give them quiet time to think.

3. Write *1 + 1* and *9 + 9* where all students can see it. Ask a few students to explain which sum is more and how they know.

   Examples of Student Thinking

   "Nine is bigger than one and one, so I don't even need to add the other nine."

   "Nine is more than one, and the second nine is more than the second one, so nine plus nine has to be more."

   "One plus one is two, and nine plus nine is eighteen; eighteen is larger than two."

4. Acknowledge that some strategies for finding which sum is larger did not include adding the numbers. Ask students to try to use the strategy for the next problem.

5. Display two more pairs of ten-frame cards:

   Pair 1: a card with eight dots and a card with five dots

   Pair 2: a card with eight dots and a card with one dot

   Ask students, "Which sum is larger?" Give them quiet time to think.

6. Write *8 + 5* and *8 + 1* where all students can see it. Ask a few students to explain which sum is more and how they know.

Example of Student Thinking

"The eights are the same, so I just looked at the five and one. And five is greater than one."

7. Summarize the discussion for students. Tell them, "When you play *Double Bank It!* again, remember to look at both sets of cards first to see if you can compare them without having to find their sums first."

Part 3: Using the Recording Sheet

1. On another day, when students are familiar with and comfortable playing *Double Bank It!*, explain to them that they are now going to record their comparisons.

2. Bring students' attention to the sentence prompts. Introduce (or revisit if students have previously played *Bank It!*) the symbols for *less than*, *greater than*, and *equal to*. Tell students, "Mathematicians write these symbols when they compare numbers." Write the corresponding symbol next to each sentence frame:

Sentence Frames for Comparing Cards

1. _____ (number or sentence) is less than _____ (number or sentence). *smaller than, not as much as, fewer than, <*
2. _____ (number or sentence) is greater than _____ (number or sentence). *more than, bigger than, larger than, >*
3. _____ (number or sentence) is equal to _____ (number or sentence). *is the same as, matches, =*

3. Write a comparison equation such as *1 + 7 > 2 + 2* and show students how to find the words that match the symbol. Point to the > sign and then to the words it represents. Read the comparison equation to the class: "One plus seven is greater than two plus two."

4. Write another comparison equation such as *2 + 2 < 5 + 4*. Ask students to look for the symbol in the list of sentence prompts and find the words it represents. Ask them to turn to their partners and compare the sums and equations using the words:

"Four is less than nine."

"Four is smaller than nine."

"Four is not as much as nine."

"Two plus two is less than five plus four."

"Two plus two is smaller than five plus four."

5. Introduce the *Double Bank It!* recording sheet (Reproducible 15). Ask a volunteer student to help you model the game using the recording sheet. You should each have a copy of the recording sheet.

6. Write your name on the left-hand side of your recording sheet. Ask the volunteer to write his name on the right-hand side of your recording sheet.

   Then, ask the volunteer to write his name on the left-hand side of his recording sheet and write your name on the right-hand side. Emphasize the importance of writing your names down in the right places!

7. Play one round of *Double Bank It!* Record the number sentences on your recording sheet, pointing out to students that you are recording the number sentence of your two cards in the first blank.

8. Ask students, "Look at the sentence prompts. Which symbol and words should I circle to correctly compare the sums?" Give them quiet time to think, then ask them to share their thinking with their partners.

9. Ask students to share which symbol or words they think you should circle. Make sure they explain their thinking. Circle their choice on your recording sheet. Have the class practice comparing the sums or the

Differentiating Your Instruction

Making the Most of the Recording Sheet
Copy the *Double Bank It!* recording sheet on both sides of the paper so that when partners finish before other groups, they can play another game by turning their sheets over.

Students who are familiar with *Double Bank It!* can record their games in their math journals or on scratch paper using the format of the recording sheet. Using their own paper means they will be responsible for writing in the comparison symbols and words; make sure the sentence frames and symbols are displayed such that all students can see and use them for support.

number sentences by reading the comparison out loud. On your recording sheet, write the sums below the corresponding number sentences. Tell students, "The space below the number sentences on the recording sheet is available for you to write the sums if you choose to."

10. Now it's the volunteer student's turn. Have the volunteer record the numbers from the cards on his recording sheet, this time recording the number sentence of his two cards in the first blank, followed by the number sentence of your two cards.

11. Ask students, "Look at the sentence prompts. Which symbol and words should be circled to correctly compare the sums?" Give them quiet time to think, then ask them to share their thinking with their partners.

12. Ask the volunteer to tell the class which one he thinks he should circle. Have him circle it on his recording sheet. Have the class practice comparing the sums or number sentences by reading the comparison out loud.

13. Repeat modeling how to use the recording sheet until students are comfortable with using it. Make sure to ask students if they have any questions.

14. Pass out one copy of the *Double Bank It!* recording sheet to each student. Make sure students still have their sets of ten-frame cards.

15. As students play the game using their recording sheets, circulate and ask questions (refer to the key questions).

Teaching Tip

Routines
The whole-class discussion during Part 4 can be used as a routine on subsequent days. This routine gives students practice with their addition facts in the context of open sentences.

Math Matters!

The equation $8 + \underline{\hspace{1cm}} > 4 + 6$ is called an open sentence because it contains at least one variable; it can be an equation that contains an equal sign, or it can be an inequality and contain an inequality sign (such as < or >). It is neither true nor false, but can be made true or false by replacing the variable with certain numbers. (See *Math Matters: Understanding the Math You Teach, Grades K–8*, Second Edition by Suzanne H. Chapin and Art Johnson, © 2006 Math Solutions.)

Teaching Tip

Agreeing or Disagreeing
Before asking students to agree or disagree with another student's answer, have a conversation about the appropriate way to agree and disagree with someone's answer. Ask students for suggestions for appropriate words to use when agreeing or disagreeing. Chart their responses and display the chart throughout the school year. Return to the chart before discussions to remind students of appropriate responses for agreeing and disagreeing.

Part 4: Summarizing the Game

1. After students have played several rounds, begin another whole-class discussion about the game.

2. Write *8 + _____ is greater than (>) 4 + 6* where everyone can see it. Ask students, "What number could make this comparison statement true?" Give them quiet time to think, then ask them to turn and tell their partners their numbers.

3. Call on several students to read the comparison statement using the numbers they discussed with their partners. Record them under the original comparison statement, this time using just the > symbol. For example:

   $8 + \underline{\hspace{1cm}}$ *is greater than (>) 4 + 6*

   $8 + \underline{10} > 4 + 6$

   $8 + \underline{8} > 4 + 6$

   $8 + \underline{4} > 4 + 6$

   After each student shares, pause and ask if the class agrees. Ask students to explain why they agree or disagree. When students find the sums of the number sentences, record those under the comparison statements:

   $8 + \underline{\hspace{1cm}}$ *is greater than (>) 4 + 6*

   $8 + 10 > 4 + 6$

   $18 > 10$

4. Now record *8 + _____ is equal to (=) 4 + 6*. Ask students, "What number could make this comparison statement true?" Give them quiet time to think, then ask them to show the number with their fingers. Record *2* in the blank space. Ask them if there is another number that could make the sentence true. Discuss why not.

5. Record *_____ + _____ is equal to (=) 4 + 6*. Ask students, "What numbers could make this comparison statement true?"

Give them quiet time to think, then ask them to turn and tell their partners their numbers.

6. Call on several students to read the comparison statements using their numbers. Record what they say under the original comparison statement, this time using just the equal sign. Your recording may look like this:

$$\underline{\hspace{1cm}} + \underline{\hspace{1cm}} \text{ is equal to } (=) 4 + 6$$

$$1 + 9 = 4 + 6$$

$$5 + 5 = 4 + 6$$

$$9 + 1 = 4 + 6$$

7. After each student shares, pause and ask if the class agrees. Ask the students to explain why they agree or disagree. When students find the sums of the number sentences, record those under the comparison statements. For example:

$$\underline{\hspace{1cm}} + \underline{\hspace{1cm}} \text{ is equal to } (=) 4 + 6$$

$$1 + 9 = 4 + 6$$

$$10 = 10$$

Consider continuing the discussion on another day; record a few more open sentences and lead students through a discussion following the same format.

Extend Their Learning!

On subsequent days, use open sentences as a routine. Tell students that you are going to play part of a round of *Double Bank It!* Draw two cards, record the number sentence and either =, <, or >, and ask students to complete the other part of the round by recording any two numbers they could draw to make the comparison true if they were playing *Double Bank It!*

Assessment: Double Bank It!

After students have had repeated experiences playing *Double Bank It!* use the *Double Bank It!* assessment (Reproducible 16) to assess their thinking in small groups or during whole group. During this assessment (similar to *Bank It!*), students record symbols, words, and a number to correctly complete a comparison statement and also have the opportunity to explain how they know which comparison symbol and words to use. If you choose to have students explain their thinking, it is important to encourage and demonstrate this skill during class discussions prior to the assessment.

Double Bank It! Assessment

Directions

Fill in the following with one of the comparison symbols.

< (is less than) 　　> (is greater than) 　　= (is equal to)

1.	9 + 3	6 + 6
2.	5 + 5	8 + 7
3.	1 + 9	1 + 4
4.	7 + 5	4 + 9
5.	4 + 3	6 + 4

Choose one problem. How do you know what symbol to use?

Directions

Fill in the following with numbers that make the comparison true.

6.	5 + 4	> (is greater than)	___ + ___
7.	6 + 1	< (is less than)	___ + ___
8.	3 + 2	< (is less than)	___ + ___
9.	___ + ___	> (is greater than)	4 + 3
10.	___ + ___	= (is equal to)	4 + 4

Choose one problem. How do you know what symbol to use?

FIGURE G-8.1 Reproducible 16: *Double Bank It!* Assessment

Game 9

Race to 20

Overview

In this game, students roll a die and place that number of counters on a double ten-frame in an effort to reach 20 first. This game builds students' understanding of landmark numbers, specifically ten and twenty. Through the use of two colors of counters, students decompose the number twenty and use number strings to compose twenty. The game also naturally lends itself to encouraging students to compare numbers. Further ideas for introducing and summarizing the game are included in the "Teacher Reflection" section. In the assessment, students use their experience with *Race to 20* to compare quantities and connect the game to number sentences.

Related Lessons

You might teach the following lessons first:

▶ R-4 Number Strings

▶ R-5 Adding Nine

▶ R-6 Sums One More Than Ten

Consider these lessons as a follow-up:

▶ P-1 Two-Color Counters

▶ P-3 Mystery Sums

Key Questions

▶ How many more counters do you need to have ten?

▶ How many more counters do you need to have twenty?

▶ How many more counters do you have compared with your partner?

▶ How would you add the counters you have so far?

Time

20 minutes

Materials

dice, 1 per pair of students

double ten-frame (Reproducible D), 1 per student

counters, 25 each of two colors per student

Extension

dice with a small sticker on one face, 1 per pair of students

double ten-frame (Reproducible D), 1 per student

counters, 25 each of two colors per student

Teaching Directions

1. Explain to students that they will be playing a game using one die and two double ten-frames. The double ten-frame is their game board; each student will have one.

2. Ask a student volunteer to help you model the game for the class. Ask her to roll the die and call out the number rolled. Then ask her to place that number of counters on her double ten-frame. Emphasize that the counters must all be of the same color.

3. Thank the volunteer student and ask her to pass the die back to you. Roll the die and call out the number rolled. Place that number of counters on your game board. Make sure you are using the same color of counters as the volunteer student did; point this out to students.

4. During the second turn, repeat the process but use the other color of counters. Ask the class, "How many more does each of us need to fill in one ten-frame or one double ten-frame?" You might also ask, "How many more do I need to have ten [or twenty] counters? How many more does my partner need to have ten [or twenty] counters?"

5. Explain to students that when a player reaches 20 (that is, fills his or her double ten-frame), he or she has won the game. Note that players do not have to roll an exact amount to win. Let students know they can place any extra counters under their game board.

6. Continue playing the game until someone wins. Once a winner has been declared, explain that students then need to record number sentences that represent their sequence of rolls. Ask students to tell you the number sentence that represents the winner's rolls

Teaching Tip

Passing the Dice
By asking students to pass the dice, you are modeling the appropriate behavior expected of them during the game. In addition, having students pass the dice in a friendly manner instead of grabbing the dice will ensure fewer disagreements.

Teaching Tip

Emphasizing Counter Colors
Make sure students understand why, on each turn, it's important to alternate between the two colors of counters. This way, they can easily see each roll depicted on their double ten-frames.

and record their ideas on the board. Then ask students for strategies to add the number string. Repeat the same for the double ten-frame that didn't reach 20.

7. Make sure to ask students if they have any questions before turning the game over to them.

8. Pass out two double ten-frames, one die, and fifty counters (twenty-five each of two colors) to each pair of students.

9. As students play the game, circulate and ask questions (refer to the key questions).

10. Summarize by choosing a focus such as the following:

   ▶ address how to figure out how many more or less you have than your partner

   ▶ work on strategies for adding number strings

Time Saver

As students are settling in for the day, ask the first two students who arrive to help with preparing the day's math materials. These students can count out groups of twenty-five same-color counters and place each group in a plastic sandwich bag. This makes it easy to distribute the counters when it comes time to do so. Alternatively, have each student count out a group of twenty-five counters in each of two colors as soon as they enter the room. Once again, they can place the counters in plastic sandwich bags so you can easily distribute the materials when the time comes to do so.

Teaching Tip

Counters
Race to 20 calls for each pair of students to have fifty counters. If you do not have enough of one kind of manipulative to accomplish this, consider letting students play pairs against pairs. Alternatively, break up manipulatives among the pairs—give color tiles to a few groups, Snap Cubes to other groups, and two-color counters to other groups.

Race to 20

Objective

Players roll a die and use counters to build that number on their double ten-frames. The player who reaches or goes over 20 first is the winner.

Materials

2 double ten-frames, 25 counters each of two colors, and 1 die for each pair of players

Directions

1. Player A rolls the die and uses one color of counters to build the number on his or her double ten-frame. Player A passes the die to Player B.

2. Player B rolls the die and uses the same color of counters to build the number on his or her double ten-frame. Player B passes the die to Player A.

3. Player A rolls the die and uses a different color of counters to build the number on his or her double ten-frame. Player A passes the die to Player B.

4. Player B rolls the die and uses the same color of counters Player A just used to build the number on his or her double ten-frame.

5. Play continues until one player reaches or goes over 20. If a player goes over 20, place any additional counters below the game board.

6. Each player records the number sentence that matches his or her rolls for the game on a sheet of paper or in a math journal. For example, if Player A rolls 5, 3, 2, 6, 3, and 1, he should then record *5 + 3 + 2 + 6 + 3 + 1*.

7. Players add their number strings to verify they match the number of counters on their double ten-frames.

Note: For each roll, players alternate the color of counters used to build the number on their double ten-frames so they can easily see a record of their rolls at the end of the game.

Homework

For homework, you can send materials and game directions home with a note attached asking the parent and child to play the game three times.

Extend Their Learning!

Place a small sticker, such as a smiley face, on one face of each die being used (typically the face showing 1). Explain to students that when they roll the die and get the stickered face, they must choose a key question to answer. Display the key questions where all students can see them. Decide if that roll will be their turn or if they can roll again.

Key Questions

▶ How many more counters do you need to have ten?

▶ How many more counters do you need to have twenty?

▶ How many more counters do you have compared with your partner?

▶ How would you add the counters you have so far?

Assessment: Race to 20

After students have been playing the game for a while, consider assessing them using the *Race to 20* assessment (Reproducible 17), which can be administered in small groups or to the whole class. Each student will need his or her own *Race to 20* assessment and access to counters or hundreds charts (Reproducible J).

The first question shows a game board with all the squares shaded in, some gray and some black. Tell the students this was a winning game board from a round of *Race to 20* and that gray and black indicate the rolls and the two colors of counters used. Ask students to write a number sentence that matches the game and show how they would add the number string together.

The second question shows two game boards, each partially filled in. Tell students this is a *Race to 20* game that is still being played and you want them to figure out who is ahead and by how much. They can use counters or the hundreds chart at their seats, but they need to show their thinking on their paper.

Teacher Reflection

My *Race to 20* Experiences

Introducing the Game

I introduced *Race to 20* by showing a class of second graders a double ten-frame and explaining that this would be the game board. I used Snap Cubes for counters.

"How can you figure out how many spaces there are on the double ten-frame game board?" I asked the class.

"I see twenty squares because two ten-frames is ten plus ten," Alex said. I wrote *10 + 10 = 20* on the easel.

"I counted by fives," Viviane said. Then she pointed to the end of each row on the double ten-frame and added, "Five, ten, fifteen, twenty."

I recorded her skip-counting on the easel and called on Timothy.

"I saw two ten boards and knew that was twenty."

"Mathematicians would record that as 'two groups of ten equals twenty,'" I explained as I recorded *2 × 10 = 20*. Even though I had not formally taught multiplication, I wanted to give students experiences with multiplication when it connected to their thinking.

I then told the students that the objective of the game was to fill up their double ten-frame before their partner filled his or hers. Each player would roll the die and place that number of Snap Cubes on the game board. I emphasized that they would use two colors of Snap Cubes so that they would be able to see the individual rolls. I called on Lucy to play the game with me and handed her a double ten-frame while simultaneously placing one in front of me.

Lucy rolled a 4 and placed four red Snap Cubes on her board. I reminded the class that it was important that the person whose turn it was handed the die to her partner when she was finished. I wanted students to learn not to grab the die before their partner was finished with his or her turn.

Lucy handed me the die and I rolled a 3. I placed three red Snap Cubes on my game board.

"How many more Snap Cubes do I need to fill up one ten-frame? How do you know?" I asked.

"You need seven. See—the bottom row has five empty and then there's two empty spaces at the top. Five and two is seven," Maria explained.

"How many more cubes does Lucy need fill up one ten-frame?" I continued the questioning.

"She needs six more. I can see five empty and one left over on the top row," Marcus explained.

Lucy picked up the die and rolled a 5. This time I instructed her to use the yellow Snap Cubes. I then rolled a 2 and placed two yellow cubes on my game board.

"Who's winning?" I asked.

"Lucy!" the class said in unison.

"How many more cubes does Lucy have on her game board compared with my game board?"

"I think she has four more cubes than you do," Marcus declared.

"How did you think about that, Marcus?"

"Lucy has the top row filled up and so do you. You need four cubes on the bottom row to be the same as her."

"Do you agree or disagree with Marcus's answer, and can you explain?" I asked the class.

"I agree! I think if you put them together, then her line will have more. I think there would be four left over," Leah explained.

I took the cubes from my game board and snapped them together to create a tower and asked Lucy to do the same. We then compared our towers by holding them next to each other. Lucy counted the leftover Snap Cubes from her tower that didn't partner with any of my cubes.

We continued the game and I occasionally stopped the play to ask "How many more?" questions. Eventually our game boards looked like this, and it was Lucy's turn to roll:

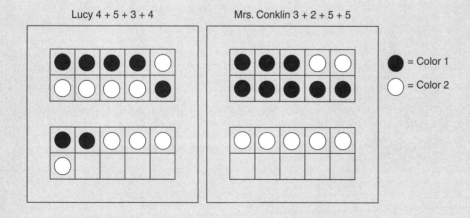

I explained to the group that Lucy could win if she rolled a 4, 5, or 6. I told them it was not necessary to roll exactly what was left on the game board. Lucy rolled a 5 and I instructed her to place five Snap Cubes near her game board.

"Lucy needs only four Snap Cubes to win, but she rolled a five. How many cubes will Lucy have left over when she fills the game board?" I asked the class.

"I think she'll have one left over. I put up my five fingers, put four down, and had one left up," Edgar said, demonstrating.

"I counted up from four and said, 'Five,' so she'll have one left over," Jamel said.

I asked Lucy to fill up her game board and check to see what was left over. She filled up the four empty spaces and held up one leftover cube. She placed it below the game board. I congratulated Lucy on getting to 20 before me and focused my attention on her game board.

"Looking at Lucy's game board, I think I can tell the story of her game. I can see what numbers she rolled each time by the color of the Snap Cubes. Is someone willing to try to tell the story of Lucy's *Race to Twenty* game?" I paused to give students time to think. I called on Javon first.

"She rolled a four, then a five, then a three, then a four, and another four," Javon said. I wrote *4 + 5 + 3 + 4 + 4* for everyone to see.

"Do you agree or disagree with Javon's idea and can you prove your thinking to us?" I prompted the class.

"I remember her rolling a five at the end of the game, but her game board shows four," Edgar said, scratching his head. "Do we say five or four in our story?"

"Interesting question. I agree Lucy rolled a five, but she could use only four Snap Cubes to fill the game board. Let me revise what I said earlier. Let's tell the story of Lucy's game board. We know that the last roll sometimes won't match what we put on the game board, so it will be the story of how her game board looks." I watched as the class nodded in agreement. "Who can prove Javon's idea of Lucy's story?"

"We can see four red cubes," Maribell moved the first four cubes from Lucy's game board to the side. "Then she has five yellow ones, and three red ones. Here are four yellow ones and four more red ones. Javon's number matches!"

"So, we have the story of how Lucy raced to twenty. Let's check the numbers one more time. Look at the number string I wrote when Javon explained Lucy's story. What numbers do you see that you can add?" I asked. The class had been working on addition strategies and number strings for a couple of weeks.

"I see some fours and I know how to skip-count by fours. So four, eight, twelve is what I did first," Marcus explained. I wrote *4, 8, 12* on the easel, then asked him what he would do next.

"Three more makes fifteen. Oh easy—fifteen and five is twenty," Marcus exclaimed, proud of himself for making his last combination "easy." I recorded *12 + 3 = 15* and then *15 + 5 = 20*.

"Thank you, Marcus. Who has another way?"

"Well I started at the end; four and four is eight, and five and three is eight, so now I have a double. Eight and eight is sixteen. Sixteen and four makes twenty," Maribell explained. I recorded *4 + 4 = 8, 5 + 3 = 8, 8 + 8 = 16*, and *16 + 4 = 20*.

"So Marcus skip-counted to help him. Maribell looked for doubles. Did anyone add the numbers another way?"

"I looked at her game board to help me," Vincent shyly contributed. I assured him that his insights were helpful and we would like to hear more about his thinking.

"Four and five is nine, and four and four is eight. I took the three and split it into a one and two, just like on her board. Nine and one is ten, and eight and two is ten, so it all equals twenty." Vincent showed the 3 on the board, split between the first and second ten-frames as 1 and 2. I was pleased that Vincent was decomposing numbers and using the game board to help him make sense of that concept. I recorded *4 + 5 = 9* and *4 + 4 = 8*. Then I wrote *3 = 1 + 2* and continued by adding *9 + 1 = 10* and *8 + 2 = 10*.

We continued by telling the story of my game board, recording number sentences, and checking to make sure those number sentences added up to fifteen.

"So today during your exploration, you will play *Race to Twenty* with a partner. When one player fills up his or her double ten-frame, the game is over and you will record the story of your game board with number sentences. Then I would like you to add up the numbers to make sure they equal the number of counters on your game board."

Exploring the Game

As students got started playing the game, I observed several groups before beginning my questioning. I have found that when I observe without interacting with the groups, I can formatively assess what they know and don't yet know. I use this information to guide my future lessons or daily routines. For example, I overheard Edgar and Leo talking about their game. They were discussing who was ahead. I heard Leo tell Edgar he was ahead of Edgar.

Edgar responded, "Yeah, but not by much."

Leo replied that he didn't know by how much, but he knew he had more. I made a note to return to the idea of how many more during the summarization of the game.

Summarizing the Game

"I noticed when some of you were playing, you would say things like 'I'm winning!' or 'I'm losing right now.' How did you know if you were winning or if you were losing?" I asked the class. I wanted to use the students' common language as a context for introducing mathematical concepts.

"When I look at our game boards, I can tell who has more because they have more filled in," explained Gabby.

I decided to fill in two game boards as an example and ask Gabby to tell us which game board was winning.

"The one with fourteen. The other one has eleven, and that is smaller than fourteen."

"Do you agree or disagree with Gabby's idea?"

"Yeah, I agree. Fourteen is greater than eleven," Leo said, nodding.

"Who can restate what Leo said in your own words?"

"Leo is saying fourteen is bigger than eleven," Javon restated.

"What I am wondering is how much bigger fourteen is than eleven. Another way mathematicians might say that is 'How much greater is fourteen than eleven?'" I wrote both questions on the easel. "When we want to find out how much more a number is than another number, we need to compare them. How could we compare the amounts fourteen and eleven?"

"We could look on the hundreds chart. See, there is eleven and a few spaces away is fourteen," Martha suggested, pointing to the chart.

"How many spaces away is fourteen from eleven?"

Martha walked up to the chart and put her finger on 11, then counted over to 14. "One, two, three," Martha said as she touched 12, 13, and 14 on the hundreds chart.

"So fourteen is three more than eleven. I wonder if we can start from fourteen and count back to eleven. Lucy, will you go try?"

Lucy placed her finger on 14 and said, "One." She moved her finger to 13 and said, "Two." Then she said, "Three," as she placed her finger on 12. When she landed on 11, she said, "Four." Lucy turned around with a confused look. I decided to get the cubes out to help Lucy and others make sense of counting on and counting back. I knew I could tell her that we don't start counting on the starting number, but I also realized she may not know why and needed to see a concrete example to help her.

I placed fourteen Snap Cubes in the middle of the rug and said, "Fourteen." Then I removed one and said to the class, "Tell me how many are in the pile."

The whole class chimed in, "Thirteen!"

I pointed to the hundreds chart and explained, "When our finger is on fourteen, that represents the whole group of fourteen Snap Cubes you see in the floor." I asked someone to explain what I did next.

"You moved one over so that we have thirteen," said Marcus.

"When I moved one away from the pile, it was the same as moving one finger over to thirteen and saying, 'One.' We are counting how many we just took away to get closer to eleven. Let's continue until we get to eleven." I stayed at the hundreds chart and asked Marcus to take another cube away.

"How many are in the pile now?"

"Twelve," the whole class said in unison. I moved my finger over to 12.

"So far, how many cubes have we taken out of the pile?"

"Two!"

"And how many spaces have I moved?"

"Two!"

Marcus took one more cube and I moved my finger one more time to 11. The class said, "Three."

"When I moved my finger, it was the same as when Marcus took one cube from the pile," I restated. I knew that I would need to revisit the idea of counting on or counting back for some students. "So, can we count back to figure out how much more fourteen is than eleven?"

"I want to try it again!" Lucy volunteered. She walked up to the hundreds chart and started on 14, then moved to 13 and said, "One." She continued until her finger landed on 11, at which point she said, "Three."

"I think you can count back," Lucy said, still seeming uncertain.

"Yeah, you can. Eleven and fourteen are in the same place. You can go forward or backward and they don't move," Maria explained. She seemed a little impatient about the amount of time we were spending counting back. I knew it was time to move on for some kids and made a mental note to work with Lucy on counting back and counting up.

"How else can we figure out how much more fourteen is than eleven?" I inquired.

"We could put the cubes together and see if fourteen is longer?" Seth suggested.

I ask Seth to snap the fourteen cubes together as I snapped eleven together. We compared them by standing them up on the edge of the easel.

I heard several students saying that fourteen was taller.

"How much taller is fourteen than eleven?"

"It has three more cubes." Seth pointed to the last three cubes in the tower of fourteen.

"If you break those off, then they would be the same," Edgar chimed in.

"You're right, Edgar, if I broke the three off, they would be equal since both would have eleven cubes. My question is How much more is fourteen than eleven? We have three strategies to help us figure that out." I labeled a piece of chart paper *How Many More? Strategies* and wrote down our strategies while summarizing them for the class. "We counted on using the hundreds chart, we counted back using the hundreds chart, and we compared Snap Cube towers. Tomorrow when you play the game, I want you to work on figuring out how many more you have than your partner or how many more your partner has than you."

Race to 20 Assessment

1.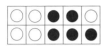

What number sentences match the game board?

$$4+1+2+3+2+2+1+2+3 = 20$$

How would you add these numbers together?

$$1+1+2+2+2+2+3+3+4 = 20$$

2. Player A's Game   Player B's Game

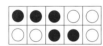   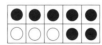

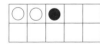   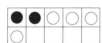

What number sentence matches the game board?

How would you add these numbers together?

FIGURE G-9.1 Jazzmine rewrote the number string, adding the smaller numbers first, followed by the larger numbers

Race to 20 Assessment

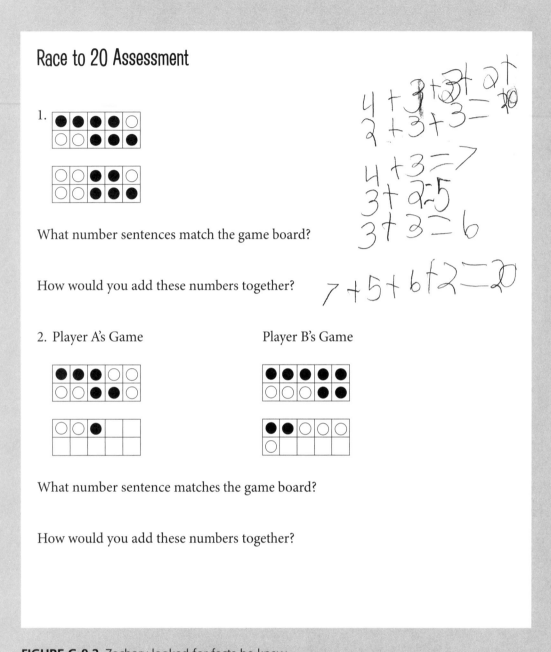

1.

What number sentences match the game board?

How would you add these numbers together?

2. Player A's Game   Player B's Game

What number sentence matches the game board?

How would you add these numbers together?

FIGURE G-9.2 Zachary looked for facts he knew

FIGURE G-9.3 For the second round, Emily began by rolling the die

FIGURE G-9.4 Chloe watched as Christian placed the counters on the ten frame. She then turned to me and said, "Christian and I both need five more counters to fill our ten-frame"

Problem-Solving Lessons Using Ten-Frames

Why these problem-solving lessons?

The lessons in this section of the book are designed to engage students in solving a problem while using a ten-frame. Some of the lessons are structured to follow a lesson plan format divided into three parts: introduction, exploration, and summary. The purpose of the introduction is to familiarize students with the problem and to connect with students' prior knowledge. This may mean solving a smaller problem or beginning to solve the problem students will work on in the exploration stage. The purpose of the exploration is to give students opportunities to discover, deepen, and extend their understanding of number. Finally, the purpose of the summary is to cement students' learning and allow students to communicate their thinking about the problem.

How much time do these lessons require?

Lessons in this section may take more than one class period. In the first period, consider introducing the problem and giving students time to explore the problem (thus working through the introduction and exploration). Begin the summary in the next math period. Reserving the summary for a later math period, rather than working through all three stages within one period, gives students time to think about the problem. In addition, students tend to be less restless and can talk longer about what they have learned when the summary takes place at the beginning of a period.

Some explorations may take two full math classes. At the end of the first day, facilitate a class discussion. Use the discussion as a means to check in with students: What do they understand? What solutions have they found? This discussion will provide support for all students when they come back to complete the problem on the second day. At the end of the second day, check in again via a class discussion. Have any new solutions been found?

If there are students who need five or ten minutes more than what has been allotted to complete the exploration, reserve time for those students to work on the problem before you begin the summary.

What is my role as teacher in these lessons?

Each stage of these lessons relies on the active role of the teacher, as follows.

Introduction

State the problem concisely. Do not tell students how to solve the problem; rather, engage students in conversation to make sure they understand what it is they are solving.

Differentiating Your Instruction

Open Problems

Some of the problems, such as P-1 Two Color Counters and P-3 Mystery Sums, are *open*, meaning more than one answer is acceptable and each student may work through the problem in a different way. Open problems give access to a wide range of learners; students who need more of a challenge can be prompted to find or organize as many solutions as possible. On the other hand, students who struggle will still likely be able to find at least one solution. Whatever the level of challenge students undertake, all students should have access—that is, they should have a way to get into the problem and work to solve it. Using open problems in math class is an exceptional way to naturally differentiate the problem-solving process and your instruction.

When students are working on an open problem and claim that they are finished, check their work closely. Are there additional answers they could discover? If so, encourage them to do so—and always keep in mind that open problems do not have just one right answer.

Because open problems have more than one acceptable answer, using a rubric to assess student thinking can be especially helpful. For your convenience, rubrics have been provided for many of the lessons in this section. These rubrics may or may not be right for you, your standards, or your grading scale; use them as a place to start and modify them as necessary to fit your classrooms needs.

Exploration

Use the key questions (provided at the beginning of each lesson) to assess student thinking and extend their learning during the exploration stage. If students are struggling with a concept, work to help them understand the problem (again, refrain from telling them how to solve it). Consider starting them on a path to solving the problem or asking them to solve a smaller or easier problem.

Summary

Facilitate a discussion on the mathematical goals of the lesson. This might include introducing or revisiting key vocabulary, looking for patterns, and making generalizations. To begin the summary, you might find it helpful to allow students to talk to their partners: How did they solve the problem? What did they learn during their exploration of the problem? Starting with partner talk allows students to feel the value of being listened to while practicing what they may say during the whole-class discussion.

After partner talk, call on a few students to share their thinking or their work (note that the goal is not to call on every student to come to the front to share his or her thinking simply because of the amount of time involved). As students share their thoughts, record their thinking where everyone can see it. This helps students make connections between mathematical thinking and the symbolic representation. In the primary grades this is especially important; repeated opportunities to see the symbolic representations will eventually help students begin to use the representations on their own.

Two-Color Counters

Overview

In this open-problem lesson, students experience decomposing numbers. Students also learn about part-whole relationships while developing an understanding of equivalent expressions. By simply changing the total number of two-color counters, you can revisit the problem several times: kindergarten students will benefit from finding combinations of five, whereas second-grade students benefit from finding combinations of twenty. The rubric at the end of the chapter can be used to assess students' progress and understanding.

For more insight into open problems, see the introduction of this section (page 157).

Related Lesson

You might teach the following lesson first:

▶ G-6 Collect Ten

Key Questions

▶ Some counters are red and some are yellow. What could your ten-frame look like?

▶ What number sentence matches your ten-frame?

▶ What if you placed three counters red side up on the ten-frame; how many counters would be yellow? Have you found that solution yet?

Time

It is recommended that more than one class period be used for this lesson. See the introduction of this section (page 157) for further suggestions for managing time for problem-solving lessons.

Materials

demonstration ten-frame (see Reproducible A)

ten-frame (Reproducible A), 1 per student

Two-Color Counters recording sheet (Reproducible 18, printed back-to-back), 1 copy per student

two-color counters (for example, red on one side and yellow on the other), 10 for the teacher and 10 per student

red and yellow crayons, 1 of each color per student

Differentiating Your Instruction

Open Problems

This is an open problem, meaning more than one answer is acceptable and each student may work through the problem in a different way. For more on open problems, see page 157.

Teaching Directions

Part 1: Introduce

1. If this is the first time you are asking students to solve an open problem, tell them, "Today's problem will have more than one solution." Explain to them that when they find a solution, you will ask them to work through the problem again to see if they can find another solution.

2. Display a demonstration ten-frame. Let students know they'll be working with seven two-color counters on the frame. Some will show red (red side up) while some will show yellow (yellow side up). How many counters could be red? How many counters could be yellow? Ask students to turn to their partners and discuss.

3. Before calling on a student, let students know you would like them to keep all the red-side-up counters together and all the yellow-side-up counters together when they place the counters on the ten-frame.

4. Ask a volunteer student to demonstrate what she thinks her ten-frame might look like. Have the student come up and place all seven counters on the demonstration ten-frame. Then ask the student, "What number sentence would match how many counters are red and how many are yellow?" As the student states the number sentence, record it for everyone to see. For example, the student might position the counters on the ten-frame as follows:

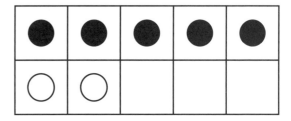

Write *7 = 5 + 2.*

Let the class know that number sentences can be written this way; since they're working with seven, you've decided to record *7* first, followed by the student's thinking.

5. Ask students, "Was anyone thinking about a different way to make seven using the two-color counters on the ten-frame?" Have a different student rearrange the counters on the demonstration ten-frame to create another number sentence. Ask the student to state the number sentence that matches how many counters are red and how many are yellow on the ten-frame. For example, this student might rearrange the counters on the ten-frame to appear as follows:

Write: *7 = 1 + 6.*

6. Repeat the above procedure with one or two more students.

Part 2: Explore

1. Explain to students that they will each receive ten two-color counters, a ten-frame, and a copy of the *Two-Color Counters* recording sheet (Reproducible 18). Their job will be to place the ten two-color counters on their ten-frame and explore what number sentences they can create if some of the counters are red and some are yellow (creating combinations of ten this time). Ask students to draw circles with crayons that match the colors of their counters on the recording sheet and to record a number sentence under the ten-frame to show their solutions.

2. Model how to complete the recording sheet by filling in the first number sentence together and then hand out the materials.

Math Matters!

The Equal Sign

Many students only see equations written like *2 + 4 = 6* or *10 – 5 = 5*. Constantly seeing and writing equations in this format leads students to develop an incorrect notion that the equal sign means the answer is coming. Change it up; try writing *6 = 4 + 2* or *5 = 10 – 5*. This helps students understand that the equal sign means that both sides should balance, or have the same value. It will also benefit students in later years when they begin to study more formalized algebraic concepts. (See *Math Matters: Understanding the Math You Teach, Grades K–8, Second Edition* by Suzanne H. Chapin and Art Johnson, © 2006 Math Solutions.)

Time Saver

As students are settling in for the day, ask the first two students who arrive to help with preparing the day's math materials. These students can count out groups of ten counters and place each group in a plastic sandwich bag. This makes it easy to distribute the counters when it comes time to do so. Alternatively, have each student count out a group of ten counters as soon as he or she enters the room. Once again, students can place the counters in plastic sandwich bags so you can easily distribute the materials when the time comes to do so. It may be helpful to have students also add crayons to their bags so all the materials are in one place and the lesson can start smoothly.

Differentiating Your Instruction

Differentiating the Process: Three Suggestions

1. If a student finds one or two solutions and comments that he is finished, ask the student to collect the ten two-color counters in his hands, gently shake them, and spill them out. Is there a solution he hasn't yet found? Encourage the student to place the counters on his ten-frame again. Tell the student to shake and spill the ten counters a few more times to see if other solutions come up.

2. If a student has almost all the solutions and comments that she is finished, see if she can find a solution using the least amount of counters red side up, the next-to-the-least amount, and so on. Or ask the student to look at her solution number sentences and try to organize the sentences in some way to figure out if she has found all the possible solutions.

3. If a student has found all the solutions, ask the student to explore different combinations of nine. Take one of the two-color counters away from the student (so he now has nine counters) and hand the student another copy of the *Two-Color Counters* recording sheet. Remind the student to color in the ten-frame and record number sentences on the recording sheet to show solutions accounting for some of the two-color counters being red side up and some yellow.

3. As students work, circulate and ask questions (refer to the key questions). (See the end of this chapter for examples of students' completed recording sheets.)

Part 3: Summarize

1. When the majority of students appear to be finished with Part 2, begin the summary of the lesson by drawing a chart titled *Two-Color Counters Problem*. Create a column labeled *Red* and a column labeled *Yellow*. Tell students you would like to organize their solutions by recording their findings in order. You will start with the least amount of red counters. Ask students, "Check your recording sheet. What is your solution that uses the least amount of red counters?"

2. Ask for a volunteer student to build her solution—the one using the *fewest number* of red counters—on the demonstration ten-frame. Have the class call out the number sentence that matches. In this case, the number sentence we are looking for is $1 + 9 = 10$; however, if students come up with additional number sentences, such as $3 + 7 = 10$, record those sentences near the chart and then ask, "Did anyone find a solution with fewer than three red counters?"

3. Record the numbers *1* and *9* on top of the chart as follows:

Two-Color Counters Problem

Red	Yellow
1	9

4. Now ask students, "Check your recording sheet. What is your solution that uses the most amount of red counters?"

5. Ask for a volunteer student to build his solution—the one using the most amount of red counters—on the demonstration ten-frame. Have the class call out the numbers that match. Record the numbers *9* and *1* on the bottom of the chart paper. Your recording should look like this:

Two-Color Counters Problem

Red	Yellow
1	9
9	

6. Now ask students, "What combinations are missing? How might we put them in order based upon the chart we've started?" Allow several students to share their thinking. It is likely that a student will mention placing the counters such that $2 + 8 = 10$ comes next.

7. As students build the missing solutions on the demonstration ten-frame, record the corresponding numbers on the chart in the proper order from least number of red counters to most.

8. When the chart is complete, ask, "What do you notice about the numbers?" Hold a class discussion on students' observations. Consider organizing solutions in other ways based upon students' thinking during the first step of the summary.

Red	Yellow
1	9
2	8
3	7
4	6
5	5
6	4
7	3
8	2
9	1

Teaching Tip

Managing Students' Time on the Problem
Some students may need or want extra time to explore the open problem. The goal is not that they find all the solutions, but that they work at their level of comfort. Be flexible enough to give students extra time if they need it; you may even consider doing the summary part of the lesson at the beginning of the next math class or later in the week.

Assessment: Two-Color Counters

I use a rubric, shown below, to assess individual student's work. First I move across the rubric from left to right, reviewing each row and circling the block in each row that applies to the student's work. Then, since each column is assigned a number of points (indicated at the top of the column), I move from top to bottom to add up the total points in each column and record them at the bottom in the *Total Points* row.

Our school used a one-hundred-point scale, so it was necessary for me to multiply the total number of points by five. While this rubric worked for me and my school, it may need to be adapted to fit your school's expectations.

Assessment Rubric

	1	2	3	4	5
	Found only one solution.	Found less than half the solutions.	Found half the solutions.	Found more than half the solutions.	Found all the solutions.
	Picture matches number sentence only once.	Picture matches number sentence less than half the time.	Picture matches number sentence half the time.	Picture matches number sentence more than half the time.	Picture matches number sentence all the time.
		Randomly solved the problem.	Organized thinking after solving the problem.	Organized thinking while working.	Organized thinking prior to solving the problem.
	Needed to work one-on-one with a teacher to solve the problem.	Needed more than four prompts and guidance to solve the problem.	Needed three to four prompts and guidance to solve the problem.	Needed one to two prompts and guidance to solve the problem.	Worked independently to solve the problem.
Total Points:					

You will need:

- A blank ten-frame
- Ten two-color counters
- red and yellow crayon

I placed ten two-color counters on my ten frame. Some were red and some were yellow. What might my ten-frame look like?

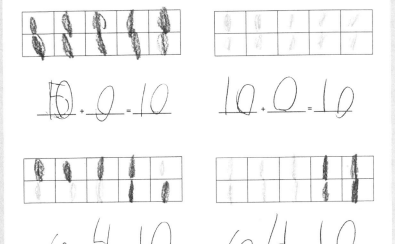

FIGURE P-1.1 Anthony systematically turned over the counters to create new arrangements and commented that they use the same numbers

You will need:

- A blank ten-frame
- Ten two-color counters
- red and yellow crayon

I placed ten two-color counters on my ten frame. Some were red and some were yellow. What might my ten-frame look like?

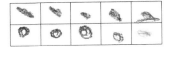

FIGURE P-1.2 Viridiana shook and spilled her counters, then placed them on the ten-frame to create different arrangements

$$0 + 10 = 10$$
$$1 + 9 = 10$$
$$2 + 8 = 10$$
$$3 + 7 = 10$$
$$4 + 6 = 10$$
$$5 + 5 = 10$$
$$6 + 4 = 10$$

FIGURE P-1.3 Jazzmine completed her recording sheet and I asked her to try to organize her number sentences

FIGURE P-1.4 While Christian recorded his thinking, Chloe checked to see if she'd written down *5 + 5* on her recording sheet

FIGURE P-1.6 Zachary had ten red and recorded *10 + 0* before turning over two and recording *8 + 2*

FIGURE P-1.5 When Matthew heard Chloe say she found *5 + 5*, he also tried to build *5 + 5*

Riddles

Overview

In this lesson, the use of riddles provides an engaging, fun avenue for students to develop number relationships, logical reasoning, and communication skills. Additionally, introducing the riddles provides an opportunity to use mathematical vocabulary. An extension is offered to help teachers write their own riddles to use with the class.

Related Lessons

You might teach the following lessons first:

▶ G-7 Bank It!

▶ G-8 Double Bank It!

Key Questions

▶ How many counters could be on my ten-frame?

▶ So far, what are the possible solutions to my riddle?

▶ How can you prove that the solution fits all the clues?

Time

It is recommended that more than one class period be used for this lesson. See the introduction of this section (page 157) for further suggestions for managing time for problem-solving lessons.

Materials

demonstration ten-frame (see Reproducible A) or double ten-frame (see Reproducible D)

ten-frames (Reproducible A) or double ten-frames (Reproducible D), 1 per student

counters, 10 or 20 for the teacher and 10 or 20 per student

Extension

containers (envelopes or sandwich bags) of several printed riddles, 1 per small group of students

ten-frames (Reproducible A) or double ten-frames (Reproducible D), 1 per student

counters, 10 or 20 per student

Teaching Directions

Part 1: Introduce

1. Introduce students to the meaning of *riddle*. Ask students, "Have you ever solved a riddle?" Read or display the farm riddle below. After each clue, ask students, "What could the animal be?" Record their thinking. As you move through the riddle, remind students to keep previous clues in mind.

The Farm Riddle	Possible Animals (Solutions)
I live on a farm.	*cow, pig, chicken, horse, sheep, goat*
I have four legs.	*cow, pig, horse, sheep, goat*
I have a snout.	*pig*

2. Now let students know that they will be solving mathematical riddles using their ten-frames. Display the demonstration ten-frame. Explain that you will be placing counters on the ten-frame, but the counters will be hidden from the students. Each line of the riddle will provide a clue about how many counters are on the demonstration ten-frame. It is the students' job to solve the riddle. Let them know you'll be giving them each a ten-frame and ten counters that they can use to help keep track of the clues.

Part 2: Explore

1. Hand out a ten-frame and ten counters to each student.

2. Remove the demonstration ten-frame from students' view. Place seven counters on it (make sure you keep it out of sight as you do this). Cover up the demonstration ten-frame so students cannot see the solution. Display the following riddle, revealing only Clue 1:

Time Saver

As students are settling in for the day, ask the first two students who arrive to help with preparing the day's math materials. These students can count out groups of ten or twenty counters (depending on whether you'll be working with ten-frames or double ten-frames) and place each group in a plastic sandwich bag. This makes it easy to distribute the counters when it comes time to do so. Alternatively, have each student count out a group of ten or twenty counters as soon as he or she enters the room. Once again, students can place the counters in plastic sandwich bags so you can easily distribute the materials when the time comes to do so.

Riddle 1

1. *My ten-frame has fewer than 9 counters.*

2. *My ten-frame has more than 4 counters.*

3. *My ten-frame has an odd number of counters.*

4. *My ten-frame has 1 more than 6 counters.*

Technology Tip

If you have access to an interactive whiteboard, type the entire riddle and use the shade feature to reveal one clue at a time.

3. Read Clue 1. Ask students, "What could be on the ten-frame?" Have three to four students volunteer their thinking. Remind them to use their counters and ten-frames to help them. Record their responses next to the first clue:

   1. *My ten-frame has fewer than 9 counters. 8, 5, 4, 1 (possible solutions)*

4. Read Clue 2 and ask students to make changes to their ten-frames if necessary. To make sure students are using both clues, have students turn to their partners and share the two facts thus far revealed about the secret number. Ask one student to share the two facts with the whole class. Have students check one more time to confirm that what they have on their ten-frames fits both fact. Circulate, checking students' ten-frames. If a student's ten-frame is incorrect, do not tell the student how to fix it. Instead, repeat each clue and ask if what the student has fits the facts. Bring the class's attention back to the displayed riddle. Ask students, "How many counters are on your ten-frames?" Record their responses next to the second clue:

   1. *My ten-frame has more than 4 counters. 5, 6, 7, 8*

5. Read Clue 3. Ask students, "What do you know about odd numbers?" Have them turn to their partners and share what they know. Ask a few students to share their thinking about odd numbers with the whole class.

6. Ask students, "Now how many counters do you think are on the ten-frame?" Remind students that their solutions must fit the first three facts. Give them time to build their solutions on their ten-frames. Ask a few students to share their solutions with the class. Record their responses next to the third clue.

7. Ask students, "Why is the number three not a solution?" Have them turn to their partners and discuss their thinking. Call on a student to share his answer with the class.

8. Ask students, "Why is the number six not a solution?" Have them turn to their partners and discuss their thinking. Call on a student to share her answer with the class.

9. Finally, read Clue 4. Give students time to think about the clue and build the solution on their ten-frames. Ask them to whisper the solution.

Part 3: Summarize

1. Tell students, "Now we are going to check the riddle to make sure seven fits all the clues." Start with the first clue. Ask, "Is seven less than nine?" Record *7 is less than 9* next to the first clue. Ask a student to explain how she knows seven is less than nine.

2. Move to Clue 2. Ask, "Is seven more than four?" Record *7 is greater than 4* next to the second clue. Ask a student to explain how he knows seven is greater than four.

3. Now read Clue 3. Ask, "Is seven an odd number?" Record *7 is odd* next to the third clue. Have students discuss how they know seven is odd.

4. Finally, read Clue 4. Record *7 = 1 + 6* and ask if students agree that 1 + 6 is 7.

5. Reveal the demonstration ten-frame so students see the seven counters.

Part 4: Explore

1. Tell students that they are now going to solve another riddle. Ask them to clear their ten-frames. Remove the demonstration ten-frame from students' view. Place three counters on it (make sure you keep it out of sight as you do this). Cover up the demonstration ten-frame so students cannot see the solution.

2. Introduce the second riddle and follow the same format used during the first riddle. Help students make sense of and explore the potential solutions for Riddle 2.

> ### Riddle 2
>
> 1. *My ten-frame has more than 2 counters.*
>
> 2. *My ten-frame has fewer than 8 counters.*
>
> 3. *My ten-frame has an odd number of counters.*
>
> 4. *My ten-frame has 2 fewer than 5 counters.*

3. Proceed with more riddles. When students are comfortable with solving riddles using the ten-frames, introduce riddles that require them to use double ten-frames and twenty counters. (Refer to the following page for additional riddle examples, including guidelines for writing your own.)

(Refer to the following page for additional riddle examples, including guidelines for writing your own.)

Teaching Tip

The Equal Sign
Many students only see equations written like *1 + 6 = 7*. Constantly seeing and writing equations in this format leads students to develop an incorrect notion that the equal sign means the answer is coming. Change it up; try writing *7 = 1 + 6*. This helps students understand that the equal sign means that both sides should balance, or have the same value. It will also benefit students in later years when they begin to study more formalized algebraic concepts.

Structure for Writing Riddles

Place the desired number of counters on your ten-frame, then use the following model to write clues:

1. Write a comparison statement using *more than, greater than, less than,* or *smaller than.*
2. Write a comparison statement using the opposite comparing phrase as the one used in the first clue.
3. Write a clue referring to a skill you want to work on, like odd or even numbers or skip-counting.
4. Write a clue incorporating an arithmetic calculation to reveal the amount of counters.

Note: For kindergartners, it may be appropriate to use only Clues 1–2 and 4.

Using a Ten-Frame

1. *My ten-frame has more than 5 counters.*
2. *My ten-frame has fewer than 9 counters.*
3. *My ten-frame has an even number of counters.*
4. *My ten-frame has 3 more than 5 counters.*

Using a Double Ten-Frame: Riddle 1

1. *My double ten-frame has more than 8 counters.*
2. *My double ten-frame has fewer than 17 counters.*
3. *My double ten-frame has a number of counters you say when you skip-count by threes.*
4. *My double ten-frame has 3 rows of 5 counters.*

Using a Double Ten-Frame: Riddle 2

1. *My double ten-frame's counters are fewer than 15.*
2. *My double ten-frame's counters are greater than 7.*
3. *My double ten-frame has a number of counters you say when you skip-count by twos.*
4. *My double ten-frame has 10 fewer than 20 counters.*

Riddle for Kindergartners

1. *My ten-frame has more than 4 counters.*
2. *My ten-frame has fewer than 9 counters.*
3. *My ten-frame's counters are 1 more than 5.*

Extend Their Learning!

Place premade riddles in containers such as sandwich bags or envelopes. Have students work in groups of two or three and give a container of riddles to each group. One student draws a riddle from the container and reads each clue, one at a time, giving the others in the group time to think about the solution using their counters and ten-frames. After one riddle is solved, students switch roles and repeat with additional riddles.

FIGURE P-2.1 Chloe listened to the first clue before placing four counters on her ten-frame

FIGURE P-2.2 After hearing the second clue, Chloe revised her thinking about the number of counters to use

Mystery Sums

Overview

In this open-problem lesson, students try to determine the mystery cards that compose a given sum. Students decompose the sum by finding various solutions for the mystery cards. The problem encourages students to find multiple solutions; more than one answer can be correct.

For more insight into open problems, see the introduction of this section (page 157).

Related Lessons

You might teach the following lessons first:

▶ R-4 Number Strings

▶ P-1 Two-Color Counters

Key Questions

▶ What cards could I be holding?

▶ Do the cards have the sum we're looking for? How do you know?

▶ The sum we're looking for is _____. Let's start with the ten-frame card with _____ dots. What other two cards can I use to make a sum of _____?

Time

It is recommended that more than one class period be used for this lesson. See the introduction of this section (page 157) for further suggestions for managing time for problem-solving lessons.

Materials

demonstration ten-frame cards (see Reproducible B), 1 set

ten-frame cards (Reproducible B), 1 set per pair of students

Mystery Sums recording sheet (Reproducible 20), 1 copy per student

Extension

demonstration ten-frame cards (see Reproducible B), 1 set

ten-frame cards (Reproducible B), 1 set per pair of students

Mystery Sums recording sheet (Reproducible 20), 1 copy

Differentiating Your Instruction

Finding Solutions

For any pair that is having trouble, draw a ten-frame card from its set and ask, "What two cards can I put with this one to make a sum of nine?" Work with the struggling pair to find two more cards to form a solution. Tell the students to work on finding another possible solution. Remind them that drawing the first card will help them get started.

Teaching Directions

Part 1: Introduce

1. From your set of demonstration ten-frame cards, select three cards that total nine. Introduce the lesson to the students by telling them they'll be solving a mystery. Point out that you are holding three ten-frame cards and the sum of the cards is nine. Their job is to figure out the number of dots on each of the three cards.

2. Pass out a set of ten-frame cards to each pair of students. Ask them to work together to find at least one set of three cards that might be the mystery cards.

3. Circulate, interacting with each pair of students. When a pair finds one possible solution, encourage them to find another.

4. Bring the students back together and ask, "Who has a possible solution for the three cards that total nine?" Introduce the *Mystery Sums* recording sheet (Reproducible 20). For every suggestion a student gives, write down the corresponding number sentence (for example, $3 + 3 + 3 = 9$) on the recording sheet.

5. After each pair of students has had a chance to share one possible solution for the sum of nine, reveal the mystery cards. Instead of acknowledging only the students who correctly guessed the mystery cards, acknowledge everyone for finding correct possible solutions!

Part 2: Explore

1. Give each student a copy of the *Mystery Sums* recording sheet. Tell students that this time the mystery cards have a sum of twelve. Emphasize that pairs need to work together and use their sets of ten-frame cards to come up with as many possible solutions for the sum as they can. When they find a

solution, they need to record the number sentence that corresponds with the three cards they've decided on. Make sure each student records the possible solutions on his or her own recording sheet. **Note:** The back of the recording sheet (should you choose to copy it that way) asks students to look for the mystery cards with a sum of fifteen.

2. As students work, circulate and ask questions. Refer to the key questions, modifying them as needed.

Part 3: Summarize

1. Ask students to review their recording sheets and share their number sentences that match the mystery cards that equal twelve. Record their number sentences where everyone can see.

2. Reveal three cards that you have chosen to represent the mystery cards that have a sum of twelve.

Differentiating Your Instruction

Using Ten-Frames

If you notice students are struggling, give them a double ten-frame and twenty counters. Draw one of the ten-frame cards from their set and build that number on the double ten-frame. Ask them, "How many more are needed so that there are twelve counters? What two cards could we use to show that number?"

For example, if you draw a ten-frame card with eight dots, place eight counters on the double ten-frame. Ask students, "How many more are needed so we have twelve counters?"

After they say, "Four," ask them, "What two cards could we use to show the four?"

If they do not reply, find the ten-frame card with one dot. Put one counter on the double ten-frame. Ask them, "How many more do we need so we have twelve counters?"

After they say, "Three," find the ten-frame card with three dots. Place the three cards in front of the students and ask them to check to make sure the three cards have a sum of twelve.

A Child's Mind . . .

Students who are developing number sense and are able to think more abstractly about number may stop using their ten-frame cards and go directly to recording number sentences. Encourage this move—it's good that they no longer need the ten-frame scaffold to help them think about number combinations!

Extend Their Learning!

On subsequent days, increase the challenge by changing the number of mystery cards from three to four or five. Use *Mystery Sums* as a routine to start math class one day a week or when there is an extra ten minutes in the day.

Assessment: Mystery Sums

I need a way to give my second graders a numeric grade when using *Mystery Sums* assessment. I've found that rubrics help me grade everyone fairly. To use the rubric below (Reproducible 21), I circle one box in each row and add the points to find a total score out of 100. If you are grading on a scale of one to four, simply change the points to one, two, three, and four. If you are using letter grades, replace the numbers with A, B, C, and D.

Use this rubric to determine a grade for the *Mystery Sums* assessment. Circle or check one box in each row.

Found no solutions. 10 points	Found 1–2 correct solutions. 15 points	Found 3–4 correct solutions. 20 points	Found 5 or more correct solutions. 25 points
Wrote none of the number sentences correctly. 10 points	Wrote less than half of the number sentences correctly. 15 points	Wrote more than half of the number sentences correctly. 20 points	Wrote all the number sentences correctly. 25 points
Was unable to use the ten-frame cards or blank ten-frame. 10 points	Used the ten-frame cards and blank ten-frame. 15 points	Used the ten-frame cards and didn't need the blank ten-frame. 20 points	Used mental math and didn't need the ten-frame cards or blank ten-frame. 25 points
Worked one-on-one with a teacher for the majority of the time. 10 points	Needed constant prompting and worked independently some of the time. 15 points	Needed a little prompting but mostly worked independently. 20 points	Needed no prompting; worked independently. 25 points

FIGURE P-3.1 Reproducible 21: *Mystery Sums* Assessment Rubric

Adding and Subtracting Ten

Time

It is recommended that more than one class period be used for this lesson. See the introduction of this section (page 157) for further suggestions for managing time for problem-solving lessons.

Materials

ten-frame cards (Reproducible B), 4 sets per pair of students

hundreds charts (Reproducible J), 1 per pair of students

pocket hundreds chart (see Teaching Tip, page 183)

Overview

In this four-part lesson, students practice adding or subtracting ten to and from numbers as well as looking for numeric and geometric patterns. Ten is an important number in the base ten system; being able to efficiently add or subtract ten from numbers improves students' mental math skills. Students get multiple opportunities to develop fluency and flexibility with number.

In Part 1 of *Adding and Subtracting Ten*, students use ten-frame cards, T-charts, and hundreds charts as they work on adding ten to numbers. In Part 2, students use ten-frame cards, T-charts, and hundreds charts as they work on subtracting ten from numbers.

Related Lessons

You might teach the following lessons first:

▶ R-5 Adding Nine

▶ G-6 Collect Ten

Consider this lesson as a follow-up:

▶ P-5 Partial Sums

Key Questions

▶ What patterns do you notice when we add or subtract ten from a number?

▶ What observations can you make when we add or subtract ten from a number?

▶ How can you use what you know about adding or subtracting ten from a number to help you solve the problem?

Teaching Directions

Part 1: Adding Ten

Introduce

1. Explain to students that this lesson focuses on adding ten to numbers. The goal is to become efficient when adding ten. Assign partners and give each pair of students four sets of ten-frame cards. (For this lesson, four sets of ten-frame cards constitute a deck.)

2. Ask students to show the number seventeen with their ten-frame cards. Each pair of students should place a card with ten dots and a card with seven dots between them.

3. Write the number *17* where everyone can see it. Next, write *+ 10* and ask students to add a card with ten dots to their display.

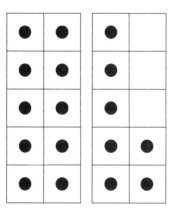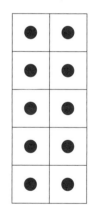

17 + 10

4. Ask partners to work together to find the sum of the three cards. Have students whisper the sum aloud. Record = *27*. Ask students how they figured out the sum. Possible strategies may be counting on from seventeen, putting the 10 cards together and adding the 7 card, or counting all dots on the ten-frame cards. Students may say, "I put the ten cards together and that makes twenty, and seven more is twenty-seven" or "I counted all the dots."

5. Ask students to show the number thirty-five with their ten-frame cards. Each pair of

---

Teaching Tip

The Word Efficiently

It is important to introduce the word *efficiently* to students and let them know the goal is for them to be able to solve problems correctly and quickly with understanding. When students know the goal and are asked to think about how they are solving problems it deepens their understanding. A note about *quickly*: *Quickly* does not mean following a rote algorithm with little to no understanding; what is quick for one student may not be the appropriate strategy for another student.

students should place three cards with ten dots and one card with five dots between them.

6. Record *35* where everyone can see it. Next, write *plus 10* and ask students to add a card with ten dots to their display.

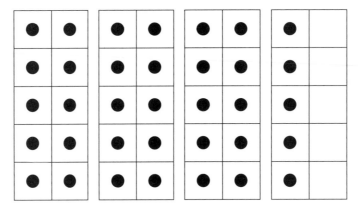

35 + 10

7. Ask partners to work together to find the sum of the five cards. Have students whisper the sum aloud. Record *= 45*. Ask students how they figured out the sum.

Adding Ten Directions

1. Use the ten-frame cards to make a number.
2. Record the number and *+ 10* on a sheet of paper.
3. Add a card with ten dots to the cards you selected in Step 1.
4. Figure out the sum and record it on your paper.
5. Repeat these directions five times, using a different number in Step 1 each time.

Explore

8. Explain the *Adding Ten* directions (see left) for the exploration part of this lesson. Display the directions for students to see.

9. Make sure students have paper to write on and ask that they work together.

10. Circulate, observing and assisting students as needed. Use the first two key questions to engage students in discussions about adding ten (see page 180).

Summarize

11. Begin the summary by asking students to bring their papers to the whole-group area. Students should leave their ten-frame cards behind; they will now be using a T-chart and the pocket hundreds chart. Draw and introduce a T-chart. Ask students to describe what this looks like. Let them know that mathematicians call it a T-chart and use it to organize their thinking.

 Technology Tip

Displaying Directions
Before class, record the directions on chart paper or an interactive whiteboard. If you use an interactive whiteboard, use the shade feature to show one direction at a time as you explain it.

12. Label the left side of the T-chart *Start Number* and the right side *End Number*. Remind students that in the exploration part of the lesson, they all added ten to numbers. The goal now is to look for patterns or make observations about what happens to numbers when ten is added.

Start Number	End Number

13. Ask a student to volunteer a number she made with her cards. Record the number on the left side of the T-chart. Then mark it on the pocket hundreds chart. Ask the volunteer student what the sum was when she added ten. Record that number on the right side of the T-chart. Mark the sum on the hundreds chart.

14. Call on four or five more students to tell the numbers they started and ended with. Each time, record the numbers on the T-chart and mark them on the pocket chart.

15. Ask students, "Look at the T-chart and the hundreds chart. What is one observation you can make?" Let them talk to their partners about their observations.

16. Ask students to volunteer their observations. As students make observations, record their thinking where everyone can see it. Save the recording of their observations; you will use it in Part 3.

Examples of Student Observations

"The end number is always bigger."

"The end number is directly below the start number on the hundreds chart."

Differentiating Your Instruction

Larger Numbers
In this lesson, a deck of ten-frame cards is composed of four sets; thus each deck has four cards with ten dots. The largest number students can start with is thirty-nine. If you would like students to work with larger numbers, add more cards with ten dots to each of the decks.

Teaching Tip

Pocket Hundreds Chart
This lesson uses a pocket hundreds chart. Pocket hundreds charts are available with all major educational retailers. If you do not have a hundreds chart, use Reproducible J in this book or insert a hundreds chart on your interactive whiteboard.

Teaching Tip

Marking the Pocket Hundreds Chart
There are several ways to mark numbers on the pocket hundreds chart. One way is by cutting a rectangle from colored construction paper that is a little taller than the number cards. Place the construction paper behind the number so both are visible. Another way to mark numbers is by using highlighter tape, available in teacher stores. Still another way is using large colored paper clips and clipping the numbers you want students to notice.

"The ones place stays the same and the tens place grows by one."

17. Tell students, "Choose one observation you heard and check your paper to see if you agree with that observation."

18. Ask a student to volunteer a number he started with but not to reveal the end number. Write the starting number on the T-chart and mark it on the hundreds chart. Ask students, "What do you think the end number will be if we add ten to it?" Allow them to think quietly. Remind them to use the observations to help them make a prediction.

19. Ask students to whisper the end number aloud. Check with the student who volunteered; is the end number right? Record it on the T-chart and mark it on the hundreds chart.

20. Repeat Steps 17–18 with several students to build fluency with adding ten to any number.

21. Introduce the *Adding Ten* prompts (see left) by reading each one aloud. Tell students that knowing how to add ten to any number will help them become efficient mathematicians.

22. Ask students to think quietly about how to complete the prompts. Remind them where the ones and tens places are in the numbers. Then have students discuss the prompts with their partners.

23. Facilitate a whole-class discussion to complete the prompts. Record students' thinking in the blanks of the prompts. Encourage students to finish the prompts by stating them several different ways, such as "Stays the same," "Doesn't change," or "Is the same number as before."

24. Cover up the pocket hundreds chart. Ask students to visualize either the ten-frame cards or the hundreds chart to help them add ten to any number mentally. Tell them, "I will say a number. You need to figure out

Adding Ten Prompts

When 10 is added to any number, the ones place _____.

When 10 is added to any number, the tens place _____.

When 10 is added to any number and marked on the hundreds chart, it _____.

what the sum is once ten has been added to it." Model a simple example by saying, "Ten." Tell students they need to add ten to ten in their heads and whisper the sum aloud when you gives the thumbs-up sign.

25. Next call out, "Thirty-two," and write it on the T-chart. Allow students to think, then give the thumbs-up for students to whisper the total aloud. Repeat with several more numbers.

Part 2: Subtracting Ten

Introduce

1. On a different day, continue the lesson by asking students to think back to when they worked on adding ten to any number. What do they remember about adding ten to any number? Have students talk with their partners, then have students share in a whole-class discussion.

2. Explain to students that in this part of the lesson they will work on subtracting ten from any number. Pass out four sets of ten-frame cards to each pair of students.

3. Ask students to show the number twenty-two with their ten-frame cards. Each pair of students should place two cards with ten dots and one card with two dots between them. Record *22* where everyone can see it.

4. Next, write – *10* and ask students to remove a card with ten dots from their display. Ask students to talk with their partners to find the difference (22 – 10 = ?). Have students whisper the difference aloud. Record = *12*. Ask students how they figured out the difference.

5. Ask students to show the number thirty-eight with their ten-frame cards. Each pair of students should place three cards with ten dots and one card with eight dots between them. Record *38*.

6. Next, write – *10* and ask students to remove a card with ten dots from their display. Ask

Teaching Tip

Visual Cues

Using a thumbs-up cue gives all students time to think. Make sure you have explicitly told students to wait for the thumbs up and remind them several times before using the thumbs-up approach.

Differentiating Your Instruction

Additional Support

If students are not successful during this section, uncover the hundreds chart for support or allow them to use their ten-frame cards so they can build the numbers.

students to talk with their partners to find the difference. Have students whisper the total aloud. Record = *28*. Ask students how they figured out the total.

Explore

7. Explain the *Subtracting Ten* directions (see left) for the exploration part of this lesson. Display directions for students to see.

8. Make sure students have paper to write on and ask that they work together.

9. Circulate, observing and assisting students as needed. Use the first two key questions to engage students in discussions about adding ten.

Subtracting Ten Directions

1. Use the ten-frame cards to make a number larger than 9.
2. Record the number and – *10* on a sheet of paper.
3. Remove a card with ten dots from the cards you selected in Step 1.
4. Figure out the total and record it on your paper.
5. Repeat these directions five times, using a different number in Step 1 each time.

Summarize

10. Begin the summary by asking students to bring their papers to the whole-group area. Students should leave their ten-frame cards behind; they will now be using a T-chart and the pocket hundreds chart. Draw a T-chart. Remind students that mathematicians use a T-chart to organize their thinking.

11. Label the left side of the T-chart *Start Number* and the right side *End Number*. Remind students that in the exploration part of the lesson, they all subtracted ten from numbers. The goal now is to look for patterns or make observations about what happens to numbers when ten is subtracted.

12. Ask a student to volunteer a number he made with his cards. Record the number on the left side of the T-chart. Then mark it on the hundreds chart. Ask the volunteer student for the difference after ten was subtracted. Record that number on the right side of the T-chart. Mark the answer on the hundreds chart.

13. Call on four or five more students to tell the numbers they started and ended with. Each time, record the numbers on the T-chart and mark them on the hundreds chart.

14. Ask students, "Look at the T-chart and the hundreds chart. What is one observation you can make?" Let them talk to their partners about their observations.

15. Ask students to volunteer their observations. As students make observations, record their thinking where everyone can see it. Save the recording of their observations; you will use it in Part 3.

Examples of Student Observations

"The end number is always smaller."

"The end number is directly above the start number on the hundreds chart."

"The ones place stays the same and the tens place decreases by one."

16. Tell students, "Choose one observation you heard and check your paper to see if you agree with that observation."

17. Ask a student to volunteer a number she started with but not to reveal the end number. Write the starting number on the T-chart and mark it on the hundreds chart. Ask students, "What do you think the end number will be if we subtract ten from it?" Allow them to think quietly. Remind them to use the observations to help them make a prediction.

18. Ask students to whisper the end number aloud. Check with the student who volunteered; is the end number right? Record it on the T-chart and mark it on the hundreds chart.

19. Repeat Steps 16–17 with several students to build fluency with subtracting ten from any number.

Subtracting Ten Prompts

When 10 is subtracted from any number, the ones place _____.

When 10 is subtracted from any number, the tens place _____.

When 10 is subtracted from any number and marked on the hundreds chart, it _____.

✚ Math Matters!

Number Sense

Helping students make connections to addition and subtraction builds their understanding of computation. It is important to help students make these connections to build fluency and flexibility with number. (See *Math Matters: Understanding the Math You Teach, Grades K–8, Second Edition* by Suzanne H. Chapin and Art Johnson, © 2006 Math Solutions.)

20. Introduce the *Subtracting Ten* prompts (see left) by reading each one aloud. Tell students that knowing how to subtract ten from any number will help them become efficient mathematicians.

21. Ask students to think quietly about how to complete the prompts. Remind them where the ones and tens places are in the numbers. Then have students discuss the prompts with their partners.

22. Facilitate a whole-class discussion to complete the prompts. Record students' thinking in the blanks of the prompts. Encourage students to finish the prompts by stating them several different ways, such as "When ten is subtracted from a number, the ones place stays the same and doesn't change."

23. Cover up the pocket hundreds chart and ask students to visualize the ten-frame cards or the hundreds chart to help them subtract ten from any number mentally. Tell them, "I will say a number. You need to figure out what the total is when ten is subtracted from it."

24. Call out, "Twenty." Ask students to silently subtract ten. Tell them they may whisper the total when you give the thumbs-up sign. Record *20* on the T-chart, give the thumbs-up, and record *10* on the T-chart after students have called out their answers. Repeat with several more numbers.

Part 3: More Practice with Adding and Subtracting Ten

1. On another day, continue the lesson by displaying the observations students made during Parts 1 and 2. Ask students what similarities or differences they notice about the two sets of observations.

2. Ask, "Would anyone like to add on to the observations?" Tell students that just as they can add 1 + 1 or subtract 1 – 1 quickly, the goal is for them to add ten or subtract ten from different numbers just as quickly.

3. Tell students, "Now you are going to mentally practice adding and subtracting ten." Display the pocket hundreds chart and ask students to visualize the ten-frame cards if needed. Remind them to keep their answers to themselves until they see the thumbs-up sign. When they see the thumbs-up sign, they may whisper the total aloud.

4. Draw two T-charts and title one *Adding Ten* and the other *Subtracting Ten*. Label the right side of each T-chart *Start Number*. Label the left side of each T-chart *End Number*.

5. Call out a number and record it on the Adding Ten T-chart. Give students time to add ten to the number. Give the thumbs-up sign. Tell students, "Now turn to a partner and share how you knew the answer." Call on a few students to share their thinking.

   Examples of Student Thinking

   Some students will use the pattern on the hundreds chart, knowing the end number comes directly below the start number.

   Some will use the place-value pattern, knowing the ones place stays the same and tens place increases by one.

   Some may visualize the cards by counting by tens and then adding the ones that are left over.

   Some may count on, still not trusting in the observations and patterns of adding ten.

6. Call out two more numbers and repeat the process.

7. Inform students that they will now work on subtracting. Remind them to quietly find the difference and wait for the thumbs-up before calling out the number.

8. Call out a number and record it on the Subtracting Ten T-chart. Give students time to subtract ten from the number and then give

Differentiating Your Instruction

Additional Support
If students are struggling with adding or subtracting ten from a number, spend more time on that operation. Consider using the ten-frame cards for additional support or handing out hundreds charts for students to use.

Differentiating Your Instruction

Alternating Between Addition and Subtraction

If students are working well on adding and subtracting ten, begin alternating between addition and subtraction. Each time, call out the number and what operation students should perform before recording it on the appropriate T-chart.

A Child's Mind . . .

Helping students make connections to addition and subtraction—such as knowing that when ten is added or subtracted, the ones place stays the same and the tens place changes—builds their understanding of computation. It is important to help students make these connections to build fluency and flexibility with number.

A Child's Mind . . .

Connecting students' thinking to the symbolic representation gives students an opportunity to see how their thinking can be represented mathematically. It also gives other students an opportunity to make sense of various strategies.

the thumbs-up sign. Tell students, "Now turn to a partner and share how you knew the answer." Call on a few students to share their thinking.

9. Call out two more numbers and repeat the process.

10. Engage students in Part 3 several times a month to build fluency with adding and subtracting ten.

Part 4: Applying Adding and Subtracting Ten

1. On another day, continue the lesson by telling students that learning to add and subtract ten quickly from any number can help them solve other problems, too. In this part of the lesson they will apply what they have learned about adding and subtracting ten to other problems. Pass out a hundreds chart and four sets of ten-frame cards to each pair of students. Tell them they may use these tools to help them in this lesson.

2. Record *12 + 10* where everyone can see it. Ask students, "What do you know about adding ten to numbers?"

3. Have students whisper the sum of 12 + 10 to their partners. Record = *22*. Under the problem, record *12 + 15*. Ask students to turn and talk to their partners about how knowing 12 + 10 can help them solve 12 + 15. Remind them that they may use their ten-frame cards or hundreds charts to help them.

4. Ask students to discuss the strategies for finding the sum of 12 + 15. Record their strategies using symbolic representations.

   ### Example of Students' Thinking and Strategies

   ▶ *"I know twelve plus ten is twenty-two, and twenty-two plus five is twenty-seven."* Record the following:

   12 + 10 = 22

   22 + 5 = 27

▶ *"I used the hundreds chart and put my finger on twelve and added ten and landed on twenty-two. Then I added five more and landed on twenty-seven."* Record the following:

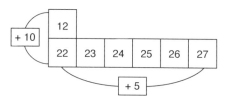

▶ *"I made twelve and fifteen with the ten-frame cards and added the tens and got twenty and added the ones and got seven. Twenty and seven is twenty-seven."* Record the following:

12 + 15

10 + 10 = 20

2 + 5 = 7

20 + 7 = 27

5. Record *33 + 10* where everyone can see it. Ask students, "What do you know about adding ten to numbers?"

6. Have students whisper the sum of 33 + 10 to their partners. Record = *43*. Under the problem, record *33 + 16*. Ask students to turn and talk to their partners about how knowing 33 + 10 can help them solve 33 + 16. Remind them that they may use their ten-frame cards or hundred charts to help.

7. Ask students to discuss their strategies for solving 33 + 16. Record their strategies using symbolic representations.

8. Write the following equations where everyone can see them:

   25 + 14

   37 + 12

   19 + 13

   36 + 18

Teaching Tip

Assisting Students with Recording Their Thinking

One way to assist students who are confused about how to record their thinking is to listen to their ideas and write their thinking on a piece of paper. Here are a few examples:

▶ If a student is trying to record counting on, and he says, "I started at twenty-five and counted fourteen on by saying twenty-five, twenty-six, twenty-seven, . . . thirty-nine," record *25* and the string of numbers he counted on.

▶ If a student is adding ones and tens and she says, "I added five and four and got nine, and twenty and ten and got thirty. Thirty and nine is thirty-nine," record either vertically or horizontally:

$$25$$
$$\underline{+\ 14}$$
$$9$$
$$\underline{+\ 30}$$
$$39$$

▶ If the student is adding on ten and then the ones and says, "I added ten to twenty-five and got thirty-five and added on four more and got thirty-nine," record either number sentences or an open number line, depending on what the class is familiar with.

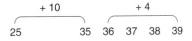

▶ If a student is using the hundreds chart to add the tens and ones, then consider drawing a portion of the hundreds chart:

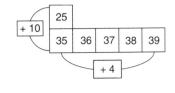

Ask students to work on the problems and record their thinking on their own papers. Remind them that they may use their ten-frame cards and hundreds charts. Also refer them to the strategies you recorded.

9. Circulate, observing students' strategies for solving the problems. When needed, assist students who are struggling to record their thinking on paper.

10. On another day, record *27 – 10* where everyone can see it. Ask students, "What do you know about subtracting ten from numbers?"

11. Have students whisper the total of 27 – 10 to their partners. Record *= 17* and under the problem, record *27 – 15*. Ask students to turn and talk to their partners about how knowing 27 – 10 can help them solve 27 – 15. Remind them that they may use their ten-frame cards or hundreds chart to help.

12. Ask students to discuss their strategies for solving 27 – 15. Record their strategies using symbolic representations.

Examples of Student Thinking and Strategies

▶ *"I took ten from twenty-seven and got seventeen, and took five from seventeen and got twelve."* Record:

27 – 10 = 17

17 – 5 = 12

▶ *"I used the hundreds chart and moved up to seventeen from twenty-seven and over five and landed on twelve."* Record:

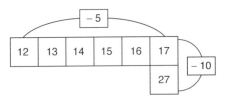

▶ *"I made twenty-seven with the ten-frame cards and took ten away and got ten, then took five away from the seven card and got two, so I had twelve left." Record:*

27 – 15

20 – 10 = 10

7 – 5 = 2

10 + 2 = 12

13. Record *35 – 10* where everyone can see it. Ask students, "What do you know about subtracting ten from numbers?"

14. Have students whisper the total of 35 – 10 to their partners. Record = *25* and under the problem, record *35 – 13*. Ask students to turn and talk to their partners about how knowing 35 – 10 can help them solve 35 – 13. Remind them that they may use their ten-frame cards or hundreds charts to help.

15. Ask students to discuss their strategies for solving 35 – 13. Record their strategies using symbolic representations.

16. Write the following equations where everyone can see them:

    25 – 14

    37 – 12

    19 – 13

    36 – 15

17. Ask students to work on the problems and record their thinking on their own papers. Remind them they may use their ten-frame cards and hundreds charts. Also refer them to the strategies you recorded.

18. Circulate, observing students' strategies for solving the problems. When needed, ask the last key question (see page 180) or assist students who are having trouble recording their thinking on paper.

19. Ask students to hand in their papers. Use their work to guide planning for future lessons. Use these guiding questions to help you think about the students' work:

Adding Ten Directions

Guiding Questions for Looking at Students' Work

▶ Are students able to talk about their strategies? If so, what vocabulary are they using? How can you reinforce mathematical language?

▶ Are students able to record their strategies? What minilessons can you teach to help move students on to more efficient strategies?

Teacher Reflection

My *Adding and Subtracting Ten* Experiences
It's OK to Ask for Help!

Teaching two-digit addition and subtraction to my second graders during my first year of teaching was the first time I realized how important it was to begin developing number sense. I realized I had not prepared them to think flexibly about numbers nor had I given them explicit opportunities to learn basic number sense that they could apply to two-digit addition and subtraction. I went to my math coach, Stephanie, and asked for help. She came in the very next day and led my students through a number talk. She gave them one two-digit addition problem to solve and then held a discussion about their strategies. What struck me was how much time Stephanie spent on one problem. I had been giving students twenty problems to solve and facilitating little discussion about what was happening. No wonder my students who were struggling kept struggling; they were not able to benefit from listening to their peers and those who had more sophisticated number sense.

After observing Stephanie teach, I made it a goal to use mathematical routines in my days for the remainder of the year. I made sure these routines built students' flexibility and fluency with number. I also made it a goal to begin the next year with the end in mind. The end for me was developing students who could add and subtract efficiently. This thinking caused me to make connections more explicit for students by recording their strategies for solving problems by drawing pictures (if they counted on their hands, for example) or writing number sentences. I also didn't wait until the unit on two-digit addition and subtraction to begin working on adding and subtracting ten from numbers.

My second revelation with my math coach came when she observed me teach. I had asked my students to solve 33 − 17. One of my students said he took 10 from 33 and got 23 and then took 7 from 3 and got 4. I calmly but

Teaching Tip

Number Talks
All of the routines in the this book are considered number talks, which are classroom conversations that center around purposefully crafted computation problems that are solved mentally. The problems in a number talk are designed to elicit specific strategies that focus on number relationships and number theory. (See *Number Talks: Helping Children Build Mental Math and Computation Strategies, Grades K–5*, © 2010 by Sherry Parrish, published by Math Solutions.)

with confidence told him, "We can't take a seven from a three." I noticed Stephanie didn't seem comfortable with this, but I went on with the lesson. Afterward, Stephanie and I debriefed about the lesson. She let me know that it is mathematically incorrect to say, "We cannot take a seven from a three." She wrote 33 and explained if we take 7 from 3 we have −4. Then if we take 10 from 30, we have 20, and 20 and −4 is 16.

$$\begin{array}{r} 33 \\ -\ 17 \\ \hline -4 \\ +\ 20 \\ \hline 16 \end{array}$$

My thinking was turned on its side. I had never seen a subtraction problem solved like this and couldn't help but think about the twenty-five students I had been telling mathematically incorrect statements to. Stephanie offered to have a discussion with my students about this thinking the next day. I was relieved and excited to see how she would handle this.

The next day during math, Stephanie wrote the problem on the board and explained that she wanted to talk about the ones place. She began by drawing a number line on the board, labeling the *0* in the middle, and labeling the ticks to the right by ones. Then she asked the students, "Do you know what would go on the left side of the zero?" Some students looked completely confused at this question, but a few raised their hands and volunteered guesses. One student said he had heard of negative numbers. Stephanie introduced negative numbers by telling them, "When it gets really cold, we can have below-zero temperatures." (We were in Houston, so these students truly could not fathom below-zero temperatures!) Stephanie also compared negative numbers to a parking garage; going below ground was the negative first floor. She labeled the number line with the negative numbers.

Then she said, "We have the three from the thirty-three, and we need to take the seven from the seventeen way from it." She placed the marker on 3 and began counting back by ones. The students joined in. When they said, "Seven," she stopped on −4. She recorded −4 and then said, "Let's work the tens place." The students all knew the answer to 30 − 10. Stephanie recorded *20*.

She then asked, "Who knows what twenty minus four is?" Stephanie gave the students time to think before asking them to whisper the answer. Then she recorded = *16*. The excitement in the room was noticeable. My students had solved the problem the day before and knew the answer was sixteen. Stephanie told them this was one more strategy for solving subtraction problems and they were welcome to try it if they could make sense of it. She reminded them that saying, "We cannot take seven from three," is incorrect because our number system includes negative numbers. She also let them know that they would not study the topic of negative numbers until later in their schooling. Of course, the statement made them beam with delight that they were learning about numbers in second grade that they wouldn't actually study until later on!

What impressed me was my students' acceptance of negative numbers. I had been so worried that this would confuse them or they would all want to solve problems this way. This was not the case; some students used the negative number method, but the majority did not. Most students used other strategies to solve the problems. However, all students began to understand subtraction in more depth.

I learned several valuable lessons that year:

▶ Just because second graders don't formally study negative numbers does not make it OK to tell them mathematically incorrect statements.

▶ Do not shy away from introducing content to students that *may* seem above them. The students who understand the strategy will use it and the students who don't understand the strategy will abandon it for strategies that make sense to them.

▶ Finally, always ask for help! As a teacher, I am constantly seeking to make sense of teaching and refine my practice. There is no better learning opportunity than coteaching with someone you can learn from and trust.

FIGURE P-4.1 Lionel discussed his thinking with Mrs. Ray

Partial Sums

Time

It is recommended that more than one class period be used for this lesson. See the introduction of this section (page 157) for further suggestions for managing time for problem-solving lessons.

Materials

demonstration ten-frame cards (see Reproducible B), 4 sets for Part 1 and 5 sets for Part 2

ten-frame cards (Reproducible B), 4 sets per student or pair of students for Part 1 and 1 set per student or pair of students for Part 2

ten-frame cards with ten dots (Reproducible C), 6 per student or pair of students

Partial Sums, Version 1 handout (Reproducible 22), 1 copy per student

Partial Sums, Version 2 handout (Reproducible 23), 1 copy per student

Extension

Partial Sums, Version 3 handout (Reproducible 24), 1 copy per student

Overview

In this lesson, students work with ten-frame cards to add two-digit numbers and record their thinking. Research on young students adding two-digit numbers has shown that many students prefer adding the tens first and then the ones. This lesson taps into this natural way of thinking—connecting students' thinking with ways to record their thinking. Part 1 focuses on addition of two-digit numbers where regrouping is not necessary. Part 2, on the other hand, uses two-digit addition problems that may require regrouping.

Related Lesson

You might teach the following lesson first:

▶ P-4 Adding and Subtracting Ten

Key Questions

▶ What is the sum of the ten-frame cards with ten dots? How do you know?

▶ What is sum of the remaining cards? How do you know?

Teaching Directions

Part 1: Adding Two-Digit Numbers

The Sum of 24 + 14

1. Explain to students that this lesson focuses on adding two-digit numbers. Give them examples of why learning to add two-digit numbers is important. One example might be the need to add the number of students in two classes so you know how many seats to have available for an assembly.

2. Display the following word problem:

> Mr. Robinson and Mrs. Williams are taking their classes to the zoo for a field trip.
>
> Mr. Robinson has ___ students in his class.
>
> Mrs. Williams has ___ students in her class.
>
> How many student tickets will they need to buy?

3. Record *24* and *14* in the blanks and write *24 + 14* on a separate piece of chart paper.

4. Show the number twenty-four using two demonstration ten-frame cards with ten dots and one ten-frame card with four dots. Show the number fourteen using one demonstration ten-frame card with ten dots and one ten-frame card with four dots.

Teaching and Technology Tip

Record the word problem on chart paper and the numbers used during the lesson on sticky notes so changing the numbers is easy. If an interactive whiteboard is available, type the problems leaving the numbers blank and use the interactive pen to record numbers for each problem.

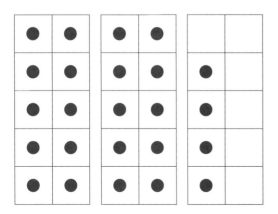
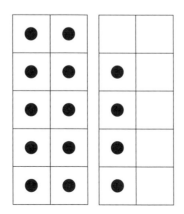

Teaching Tip

Recording Horizontally and Vertically
All teachers have to decide whether they will record two-digit addition problems horizontally or vertically or both. Writing the equations horizontally places the focus on place value. Students see the two-digit numbers decomposed into their place-value parts. It also connects to the language students are expected to use. When they say, "I added twenty and ten and got thirty," they see *20 + 10 = 30* instead of just seeing the 2, the 1, and the 3 in the tens column. When you are first introducing two-digit addition, it can be helpful to record both ways and ultimately allow students to choose which recording method makes the most sense to them.

5. Ask students, "What is the sum of all the cards with ten dots?" Give them time to think before asking them to whisper the sum aloud. Move all the ten-frame cards with ten dots together and record *30*. Ask a few students to describe how they figured out the sum and choose to record the computations in one of the two formats, as shown below.

Examples of Student Thinking

"I counted by tens: ten, twenty, thirty."

"I counted on from twenty: twenty, thirty."

$$24$$
$$\underline{+\ 14}$$
$$30$$

$$24 + 14 =$$
$$20 + 10 = 30$$

6. Next ask students, "What is the sum of four plus four?" Give students time to think before asking them to whisper the sum aloud. Move the two ten-frame cards with four dots together and record the number sentence. Ask a few students to describe how they figured out the sum.

Examples of Student Thinking

"I knew four plus four equals eight because I know my doubles."

"I counted from four: four, five, six, seven, eight."

$$24$$
$$\underline{+\ 14}$$
$$30$$
$$\underline{+\ 8}$$

$$24 + 14 =$$
$$20 + 10 = 30$$
$$4 + 4 = 8$$

7. Ask students, "What is the sum of thirty and eight?" Give students time to think before asking them to whisper the sum aloud. Finish recording the computation. Ask a few students to describe how they figured out the sum.

Examples of Student Thinking

"I just know thirty and eight is thirty-eight, because you're adding eight to a zero."

"I counted on from thirty: thirty, thirty-one, thirty-two, . . . thirty-eight."

$$24$$
$$\underline{+\ 14}$$
$$30$$
$$\underline{+\ 8}$$
$$38$$

$$24 + 14 =$$
$$20 + 10 = 30$$
$$4 + 4 = 8$$
$$30 + 8 = 38$$

8. Summarize by pointing out that they found the sum of *24 + 14* by adding the tens and then adding the ones that were left over. The sum of twenty-four and fourteen is thirty-eight.

The Sum of 35 + 12

9. Pass out four sets of ten-frame cards and six extra ten-frame cards with ten dots to each student or pair of students. Tell students you would like them to work with the cards to solve several more two-digit problems.

10. Replace the numbers in the word problem with *35* and *12*.

11. Show the number thirty-five using three demonstration ten-frame cards with ten dots and one ten-frame card with five dots. Show the number twelve using one demonstration ten-frame card with ten dots and one ten-frame card with two dots.

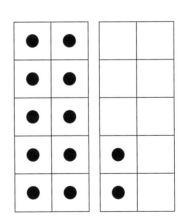

12. Ask students to build the numbers thirty-five and twelve using their sets of ten-frame cards.

Mr. Robinson and Mrs. Williams are taking their classes to the zoo for a field trip.

Mr. Robinson has ___ students in his class.

Mrs. Williams has ___ students in her class.

How many student tickets will they need to buy?

13. Ask students, "What is the sum of your cards with ten dots?" Give them time to think before asking them to whisper the sum aloud. Move all the ten-frame cards with ten dots together and record the equation choosing either the vertical or horizontal recording method.

35	$35 + 12 =$
$\underline{+\ 12}$	$30 + 10 = 40$
40	$5 + 2 = 7$
$\underline{+\ 7}$	$40 + 7 = 47$
47	

14. Ask a few students to describe how they figured out the sum.

15. Next ask students, "What is the sum of the last two cards?" Give them time to think before asking them to whisper the sum aloud. Move the two cards together and record $5 + 2 = 7$. Ask a few students to describe how they figured out the sum.

16. Ask students, "What is the sum of forty and seven?" Give students time to think before asking them to whisper the sum aloud. Ask a few students to describe how they figured out the sum.

17. Summarize by pointing out that they found the sum of $35 + 12$ by adding the tens and then adding the ones that were left over. The sum of thirty-five and twelve is forty-seven.

The Sum of 23 + 26

18. Replace the numbers in the word problem with 23 and 26. Ask students to build the numbers using their ten-frame cards.

19. Circulate, observing and assisting students as needed. When students have had time to build the numbers, ask them to turn to their partners and share what cards they used to build the numbers. Call on a student to share what cards she used for the number twenty-three; she may say, "When

Mr. Robinson and Mrs. Williams are taking their classes to the zoo for a field trip.

Mr. Robinson has ___ students in his class.

Mrs. Williams has ___ students in her class.

How many student tickets will they need to buy?

I made twenty-three, I used two ten cards and a three card." Next ask another student to share what cards he used for the number twenty-six; he may say, "When I made twenty-six I used two groups of ten cards and the six card." Using the demonstration ten-frame cards, build the numbers as students contribute their thinking.

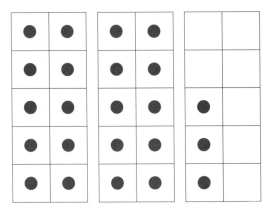

20. Ask students, "What is the sum of all your cards with ten dots?" Have them tell their partners the sum. Then ask them to whisper the sum aloud. Record *23 + 26* and add *40* underneath.

21. Next ask students, "What is the sum of the last two cards?" Give them time to think before asking them to whisper the sum aloud. Move the remaining two demonstration ten-frame cards together and record *3 + 6 = 9*.

22. Finally, ask the students to find the sum of forty and nine and tell their partners. Have the class whisper the sum aloud. Record *49*. Your final record should look something like this:

23	*23 + 26 =*
+ 26	*20 + 20 = 40*
40	*3 + 6 = 9*
+ 9	*40 + 9 = 49*
49	

23. Summarize by pointing out that they found the sum of *23 + 26* by adding the ten-frame cards with ten dots and then adding the cards that were left over.

Teaching Tip

Verbalizing Mathematical Language
By asking students to discuss what cards they used, you give them the opportunity to practice verbalizing place-value vocabulary.

Teaching Tip

Modeling with Students

Ask students to work through one problem with you. It may also be helpful to list these simple directions for students to refer to.

1. Use the ten-frames to build the two numbers.
2. Add the tens cards and record a number sentence.
3. Add the ones cards and record a number sentence.
4. Find the sum and record a final number sentence.

Differentiating Your Instruction

Mental Math

For students who need more of a challenge, ask them if they can mentally think about adding the tens and ones instead of physically using the cards. Talk through a problem with those students. For example, for the problem *34 + 13*, ask the students, "How many cards with ten dots would be used to build thirty-four and thirteen? Visualize the cards in your head." Follow up by asking if they know the sum of thirty and ten. If the students know, tell them to write it on their handouts. Next ask if they know how many leftovers there would be and what the sum would be of those two numbers. If the students know, tell them to write it on their handouts. Finally, ask them if they can find the sum of forty and seven and tell them to write it on their papers.

24. Explain to students that they will now work on a few more problems. Pass out one copy of the *Partial Sums, Version 1* handout (Reproducible 22) to each student. Do the first problem together as a class and model what is expected of students.

25. As students work, circulate and ask questions (refer to the key questions).

Part 2: Adding Two-Digit Numbers by Regrouping

1. On another day, begin Part 2 by referring to a problem from Part 1, for example, 23 + 26. Tell students that in the problem, the sum of the ones that were left over was less than ten. Model solving 23 + 26 to demonstrate 3 + 6 = 9. Let students know that now they will explore adding two-digit numbers when the sum of the ones that are left over is more than ten.

The Sum of 36 + 15

2. Display the following word problem:

> Mr. Robinson and Mrs. Williams's classes are collecting soda cans for the school recycling program.
>
> Mr. Robinson's class has collected ___ soda cans in one week.
>
> Mrs. Williams's class has collected ___ soda cans.
>
> How many total soda cans have Mr. Robinson and Mrs. Williams's classes collected?

3. Record *36* and *15* in the blanks and write *36 + 15* on a separate piece of chart paper. Show the number thirty-six using three demonstration ten-frame cards with ten dots and one ten-frame card with six dots. Show the number fifteen using one demonstration ten-frame card with ten dots and one ten-frame card with five dots.

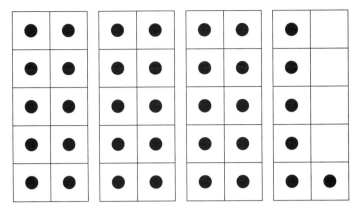 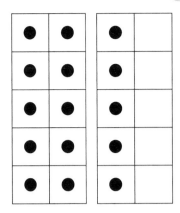

4. Ask students, "What is the sum of all your cards with ten dots?" Give them time to think before asking them to whisper the sum aloud. Move the demonstration ten-frame cards together and record *40* under *36 + 15*. Ask a few students to explain how they figured out the sum. You may hear comments such as "I added ten to thirty and got forty" and "I counted by tens: ten, twenty, thirty, forty."

$$
\begin{array}{l}
36 \\
\underline{+\ 15} \\
40
\end{array}
\qquad
\begin{array}{l}
36 + 15 = \\
30 + 10 = 40
\end{array}
$$

5. Next ask students, "What is the sum of the last cards?" Give them time to think before asking them to whisper the sum aloud. Move the two remaining demonstration ten-frame cards together and record:

$$
\begin{array}{l}
36 \\
\underline{+\ 15} \\
40 \\
\underline{+\ 11}
\end{array}
\qquad
\begin{array}{l}
36 + 15 = \\
30 + 10 = 40 \\
6 + 5 = 11
\end{array}
$$

Ask a few students to describe how they figured out the sum.

6. Now students must combine the partial sums forty and eleven. Explain that they could combine the tens again. Ask students, "How can you build eleven starting with your ten card?" Ask how many ones would be left over. Give students time to think

about which cards they would use and then call on a student to explain. Model replacing the card with six dots and the card with five dots with a card with ten dots and a card with one dot.

7. Ask students, "What is the sum of all your cards with ten dots?" Give them time to think before asking them to whisper the sum aloud. Move all the demonstration ten-frame cards with ten dots together, then refer to the remaining card, the card with one dot, and record:

36	36 + 15 =
+ 15	30 + 10 = 40
40	6 + 5 = 11
+ 11	40 + 10 = 50
50	50 + 1 =
+ 1	

8. Finally, ask the students to whisper the sum of *50 + 1*. Record *51*.

9. Record the number sentences again. Ask students to think about another way of combining the partial sums.

36	36 + 15 =
+ 15	30 + 10 = 40
40	6 + 5 = 11
+ 11	

Examples of Student Thinking

▸ *"I know that forty and eleven are fifty-one because those are two friendly numbers."*

36	36 + 15 =
+ 15	30 + 10 = 40
40	6 + 5 = 11
+ 11	40 + 11 = 51
51	

▶ *"I know zero and one is one, and four and one is five, so it's fifty-one." (If the student refers to forty and ten as four and one, use the ten-frame cards to discuss the meaning of forty and ten with the class. Rephrase the student's thinking as "You know zero and one is one, and four tens and one ten is five tens.")*

$$36$$
$$\underline{+\ 15}$$
$$40$$
$$\underline{+\ 11}$$
$$51$$

$$36 + 15 =$$
$$30 + 10 = 40$$
$$6 + 5 = 11$$

$$40 + 10 = 50$$
$$1 + 50 = 51$$

The Sum of 27 + 16

10. Give each student or pair of students four sets of ten-frame cards and six extra ten-frame cards with ten dots. Tell students you would like them to work with the cards to solve several more two-digit problems.

11. Replace the numbers in the word problem with *27* and *16*. Ask students to build the numbers using their ten-frame cards.

12. Circulate, observing and assisting students as needed. When students have had time to build the numbers, call on a student to share what cards she used for the number twenty-seven. Next ask another student to share what cards he used for the number sixteen.

Mr. Robinson and Mrs. Williams's classes are collecting soda cans for the school recycling program.

Mr. Robinson's class has collected ___ soda cans in one week.

Mrs. Williams's class has collected ___ soda cans.

How many total soda cans have Mr. Robinson and Mrs. Williams's classes collected?

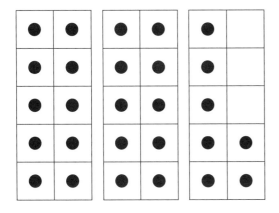

Using the demonstration ten-frame cards, build the numbers as students contribute their thinking. Record *27 + 16*.

13. Ask students, "What is the sum of all your cards with ten dots?" Have students tell their partners, then have them whisper the sum aloud. Record the sum of *30*.

14. Next ask students, "What is the sum of the cards you have left?" Have students tell their partners, then have them whisper the sum aloud. Record the sum of *13*.

27	27 + 16 =
+ 16	20 + 10 = 30
30	7 + 6 = 13
+ 13	

15. Give students the option of trading their card with seven dots and their card with six dots for a card with ten dots and a card with three dots. They may also add numbers mentally.

16. Ask students, "How would you add thirty plus thirteen?" Have them talk to their partners about their strategies. Call on a few students to share their thinking.

27	27 + 16 =
+ 16	20 + 10 = 30
30	7 + 6 = 13
+ 13	

Examples of Student Thinking

▶ *"I added the ten cards and got forty, and three was left over. Forty and three is forty-three."*

▶ *"I added zero and three and got three. I added three tens and one ten and got four tens, so it's forty-three."*

27	27 + 16 =
+ 16	20 + 10 = 30
30	7 + 6 = 13
+ 13	30 + 13 = 43
43	

Additional Problems

17. Repeat Steps 11–16, each time replacing the numbers in the word problem with one of the following sets:

    34 and 28

    49 and 23

    27 and 35

    For each problem, model recording the number sentences.

Using the *Partial Sums, Version 2* Handout

18. Explain to students that they will work on a few more problems. Pass out one copy of the *Partial Sums, Version 2* handout (Reproducible 23) to each student. Work through the first problem together to model what is expected of students. As students work, circulate and ask questions (refer to the key questions).

Mr. Robinson and Mrs. Williams's classes are collecting soda cans for the school recycling program.

Mr. Robinson's class has collected ____ soda cans in one week.

Mrs. Williams's class has collected ____ soda cans.

How many total soda cans have Mr. Robinson and Mrs. Williams's classes collected?

Extend Their Learning!

If students finish early, allow them to choose the numbers for the word problems on the *Partial Sums, Version 3* handout (Reproducible 24).

As another option, ask students to write their own word problems using two-digit numbers and find the sums.

Differentiating Your Instruction

Offering Choice
Giving students choice allows them to work with numbers that are right for them. Choice motivates learners and builds autonomy.

FIGURE P-5.1 During *Partial Sums*, Part 1, Juliana added the cards with ten dots first

FIGURE P-5.2 During *Partial Sums*, Part 2, Angel said he counted by tens then skipped over the six so he could add the tens first

Reproducibles

The following reproducibles are referenced and used with individual Routines, Games, and Problem-Solving Activities:

Reproducible 1 Number Strings Recording Sheet

Reproducible 2 Adding Nine Recording Sheet

Reproducible 3 Adding Nine Assessment Checklist

Reproducible 4 Sums of More Than Ten Cards, Version 1

Reproducible 5 Sums of More Than Ten Cards, Version 2

Reproducible 6 Sums of More Than Ten Recording Sheet

Reproducible 7 Spinner

Reproducible 8 More or Less Recording Sheet

Reproducible 9 Make Five Recording Sheet

Reproducible 10 Secret Card Assessment Rubric

Reproducible 11 Collect Ten Recording Sheet

Reproducible 12 Collect Ten Assessment

Reproducible 13 Bank It! Recording Sheet

Reproducible 14 Bank It! Assessment

Reproducible 15 Double Bank It! Recording Sheet

Reproducible 16 Double Bank It! Assessment

Reproducible 17 Race to 20 Assessment

Reproducible 18 Two-Color Counters Recording Sheet

Reproducible 19 Mystery Sums, Version 1

Reproducible 20 Mystery Sums, Version 2

Reproducible 21 Mystery Sums Assessment Rubric

Reproducible 22 Partial Sums, Version 1

Reproducible 23 Partial Sums, Version 2

Reproducible 24 Partial Sums, Version 3

The following reproducibles are referenced and used throughout the book:

Reproducible A   Ten-Frame

Reproducible B   Ten-Frame Cards

Reproducible C   Ten-Frame Cards with Ten Dots

Reproducible D   Double Ten-Frames

Reproducible E   Dot Cards

Reproducible F   Numeral Cards

Reproducible G   Computation Cards, Set A

Reproducible H   Computation Cards, Set B

Reproducible I   Computation Cards, Set C

Reproducible J   Hundreds Chart

Number Strings Recording Sheet

Name: _____

Directions

Find the sums for the following number strings. You may use a set of ten-frame cards and/or a double ten-frame and counters to help you.

1. $2 + 6 + 4$

2. $5 + 3 + 8$

3. $8 + 4 + 2$

4. $7 + 5 + 3$

5. $5 + 4 + 1$

6. $1 + 6 + 9$

7. $5 + 8 + 5$

8. $7 + 2 + 6$

9. $9 + 3 + 7$

10. $8 + 9 + 1$

Adding Nine Recording Sheet

Name: _____

Directions

1. Look at the problem. Use counters to build the first number sentence on your double ten-frame.

2. Make a ten on your double ten-frame by rearranging the counters you've placed, and complete the second number sentence.

3. Figure out the sum. Record the sum for both sentences.

1. $9 + 7 = 10 +$ _____

_____ = _____

2. $9 + 2 = 10 +$ _____

_____ = _____

3. $9 + 8 = 10 +$ _____

_____ = _____

4. $9 + 4 =$ _____ $+$ _____

_____ = _____

5. $9 + 6 =$ _____ $+$ _____

_____ = _____

6. $9 + 5 =$ _____ $+$ _____

_____ = _____

7. $9 + 1 =$ _____ $+$ _____

_____ = _____

8. $9 + 3 =$ _____ $+$ _____

_____ = _____

Adding Nine Assessment Checklist

Name: _____

Adding 9 Fact	Knew Instantly or with a Small Amount of Thinking	Used a Strategy Like Making a Ten	Used a Counting Strategy Like Counting on or Counting All	Called Out the Wrong Answer (Record the child's answer in the box.)	Could Not Figure Out

Sums of More Than Ten Cards, Version 1

Name: _____

7 + 5 =	5 + 6 =
4 + 8 =	8 + 7 =
9 + 3 =	9 + 7 =
7 + 4 =	6 + 7 =
9 + 6 =	8 + 5 =

Sums of More Than Ten Cards, Version 2

Name: _____

8 + 3 =	5 + 8 =
4 + 9 =	9 + 5 =
7 + 8 =	9 + 7 =
5 + 7 =	4 + 7 =
8 + 9 =	6 + 5 =

Sums of More Than Ten Recording Sheet

Name: _____

Directions

1. Turn over the top *Sums of More Than Ten* card in your pile and record the number sentence.

2. Use counters to build the number sentence on your double ten-frame.

3. Make a ten by rearranging the counters you've placed and record the new number sentence.

4. Figure out the sum. Record the sum for both sentences.

1. _____ + _____ = _____ + _____

                    _____ = _____

2. _____ + _____ = _____ + _____

                    _____ = _____

3. _____ + _____ = _____ + _____

                    _____ = _____

4. _____ + _____ = _____ + _____

                    _____ = _____

(continued)

(Sums of More Than Ten Recording Sheet, *continued*)

5. _____ + _____ = _____ + _____

_____ = _____

6. _____ + _____ = _____ + _____

_____ = _____

7. _____ + _____ = _____ + _____

_____ = _____

8. _____ + _____ = _____ + _____

_____ = _____

9. _____ + _____ = _____ + _____

_____ = _____

10. _____ + _____ = _____ + _____

_____ = _____

Spinner

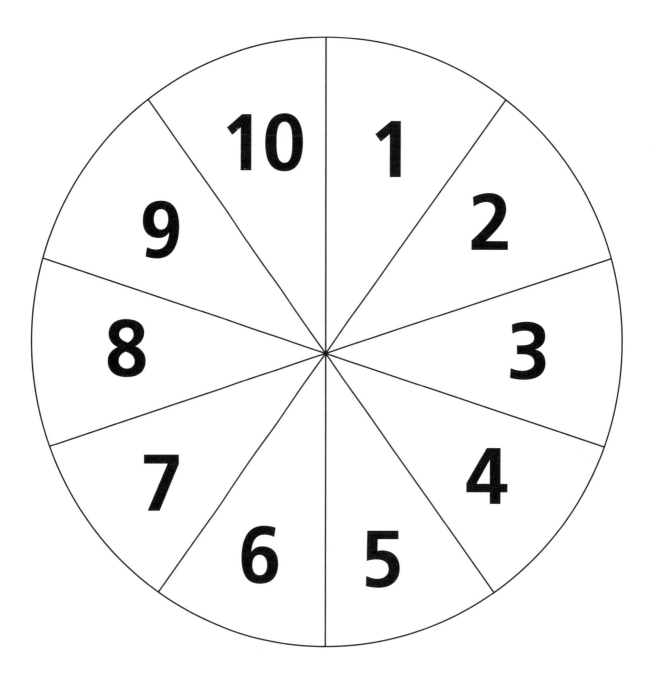

1. Pass out 1 large paper clip.

2. Use the tip of a pencil to keep the paper clip on the spinner.

3. Spin the paper clip while holding the pencil or have a partner hold the pencil while you spin the paper clip.

More or Less Recording Sheet

Name: _____

Directions

1. In the first blank, record the number of squares on the ten-frame with counters.

2. In the second blank, record the number of squares without counters (empty squares).

3. Then add the numbers together and record the sum in the third blank.

1. _____ + _____ = _____   6. _____ + _____ = _____

2. _____ + _____ = _____   7. _____ + _____ = _____

3. _____ + _____ = _____   8. _____ + _____ = _____

4. _____ + _____ = _____   9. _____ + _____ = _____

5. _____ + _____ = _____   10. _____ + _____ = _____

Make Five Recording Sheet

Name: _____

Directions

1. For each pair of cards you collect, write the number of the first card in the first blank, then write the number of the second card in the second blank.

2. Finally, fill in the sum in the third blank. (**Note:** If you get a 5 card, record either 5 + 0 = 5 or 5 = 5.)

1. _____ + _____ = _____   6. _____ + _____ = _____

2. _____ + _____ = _____   7. _____ + _____ = _____

3. _____ + _____ = _____   8. _____ + _____ = _____

4. _____ + _____ = _____   9. _____ + _____ = _____

5. _____ + _____ = _____   10. _____ + _____ = _____

Secret Card Assessment Rubric

Name: _____

Secret Number (Ask out of order.)	Knows the Secret Number Instantly	Uses a Counting Strategy to Figure Out the Secret Number and Is Correct	Uses a Counting Strategy to Figure Out the Secret Number and Is Incorrect	Guesses the Secret Number
0				
1				
2				
3				
4				
5				

Collect Ten Recording Sheet

Name: _____

Directions

1. For each pair of cards you collect, write the number of the first card in the first blank, then write the number of the second card in the second blank.

2. Finally, fill in the sum in the third blank.

3. At the end of the game, complete the sentence frames at the bottom of the page.

1. _____ + _____ = _____   10. _____ + _____ = _____

2. _____ + _____ = _____   11. _____ + _____ = _____

3. _____ + _____ = _____   12. _____ + _____ = _____

4. _____ + _____ = _____   13. _____ + _____ = _____

5. _____ + _____ = _____   14. _____ + _____ = _____

6. _____ + _____ = _____   15. _____ + _____ = _____

7. _____ + _____ = _____   16. _____ + _____ = _____

8. _____ + _____ = _____   17. _____ + _____ = _____

9. _____ + _____ = _____   18. _____ + _____ = _____

My total for *Collect Ten* is _____.

My total of _____ is _____ than my partner's total of _____.

Collect Ten Assessment

Name: _____

1. I was playing *Collect Ten* with a friend. My hand looked like this:

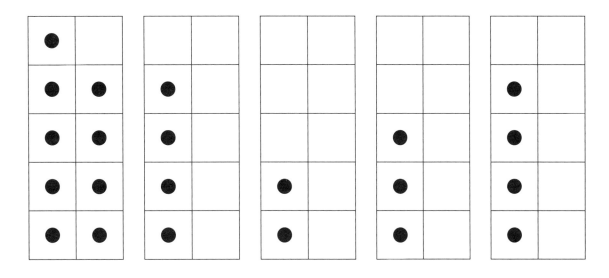

   What card should I ask my friend for? Why?

2. Look at my cards from Question 1. What card should I ask for on my next turn? Why?

(continued)

3. My friend asked me for an 8. What card do you think she will match it with to make a sum of 10? How do you know? Use words, numbers, or pictures to explain your thinking.

4. My friend asked for a 3. What card do you think she will match it with to make a sum of 10? How do you know? Use words, numbers, or pictures to explain your thinking.

5. What math did you learn from playing *Collect Ten*?

Bank It! Recording Sheet

Your Name: _____ **Your Partner's Name:** _____

Directions

For each turn, record the number of your card in the first blank, then record the number of your partner's card in the second blank. Finally, circle the symbol and words that correctly compare the numbers.

Circle one:

1. _____

    < (less than)   _____

    > (greater than)

    = (equal to)

2. _____

    < (less than)   _____

    > (greater than)

    = (equal to)

3. _____

    < (less than)   _____

    > (greater than)

    = (equal to)

4. _____

    < (less than)   _____

    > (greater than)

    = (equal to)

(continued)

Circle one:

5. _____

< (less than)

> (greater than)

= (equal to)

_____

6. _____

< (less than)

> (greater than)

= (equal to)

_____

7. _____

< (less than)

> (greater than)

= (equal to)

_____

8. _____

< (less than)

> (greater than)

= (equal to)

_____

9. _____

< (less than)

> (greater than)

= (equal to)

_____

10. _____

< (less than)

> (greater than)

= (equal to)

_____

Bank It! Assessment

Name: _____

Directions

Fill in the following with one of the comparison symbols and explain your thinking below.

< (is less than)   > (is greater than)   = (is equal to)

1.	9	6
2.	5	8
3.	1	1
4.	7	5
5.	4	6

Choose one problem. How do you know what symbol to use?

Directions

Fill in the following with a number that makes the comparison true and explain your thinking below.

< (is less than)   > (is greater than)   = (is equal to)

6.	8	> (is greater than)	___
7.	6	< (is less than)	___
8.	3	< (is less than)	___
9.	2	> (is greater than)	___
10.	7	= (is equal to)	___

Choose one problem. How do you know what number to use?

Double Bank It! Recording Sheet

Your Name: _____ **Your Partner's Name:** _____

Directions

For each turn:

1. Record the number sentence for your two cards in the first two blanks.

2. Record the number sentence for your partner's two cards in the third and fourth blanks.

3. Circle the symbol and words that correctly compare the number sentences. You may write the sum of each number sentence underneath the blanks if you want.

Circle one:

1. _____ + _____   < (less than)   _____ + _____

   > (greater than)

   = (equal to)

2. _____ + _____   < (less than)   _____ + _____

   > (greater than)

   = (equal to)

3. _____ + _____   < (less than)   _____ + _____

   > (greater than)

   = (equal to)

(continued)

4. _____ + _____   < (less than)   _____ + _____

                                       > (greater than)

                                       = (equal to)

5. _____ + _____   < (less than)   _____ + _____

                                       > (greater than)

                                       = (equal to)

6. _____ + _____   < (less than)   _____ + _____

                                       > (greater than)

                                       = (equal to)

7. _____ + _____   < (less than)   _____ + _____

                                       > (greater than)

                                       = (equal to)

8. _____ + _____   < (less than)   _____ + _____

                                       > (greater than)

                                       = (equal to)

9. _____ + _____   < (less than)   _____ + _____

                                       > (greater than)

                                       = (equal to)

10. _____ + _____   < (less than)   _____ + _____

                                       > (greater than)

                                       = (equal to)

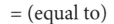

Double Bank It! Assessment

Name: _____

Directions

Fill in the following with one of the comparison symbols.

< (is less than)   > (is greater than)   = (is equal to)

1. 9 + 3   6 + 6

2. 5 + 5   8 + 7

3. 1 + 9   1 + 4

4. 7 + 5   4 + 9

5. 4 + 3   6 + 4

Choose one problem. How do you know what symbol to use?

Directions

Fill in the following with numbers that make the comparison true.

6. 5 + 4   > (is greater than)   ___ + ___

7. 6 + 1   < (is less than)   ___ + ___

8. 3 + 2   < (is less than)   ___ + ___

9. ___ + ___   > (is greater than)   4 + 3

10. ___ + ___   = (is equal to)   4 + 4

Choose one problem. How do you know what symbol to use?

Race to 20 Assessment

Name: _____

1.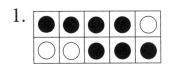

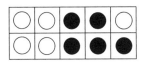

What number sentences match the game board?

How would you add these numbers together?

2. Player A's Game   Player B's Game

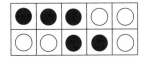   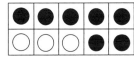

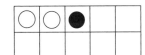   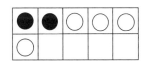

What number sentence matches the game board?

How would you add these numbers together?

Two-Color Counters Recording Sheet

Name: _____

You will need:

- 1 ten–frame

- 10 two–color counters

- 1 red and 1 yellow crayon

I placed ten two-color counters on my ten frame. Some were red and some were yellow. What might my ten-frame look like?

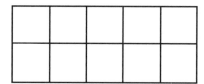

_____ + _____ = _____   _____ + _____ = _____

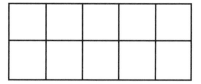

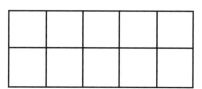

_____ + _____ = _____   _____ + _____ = _____

(continued)

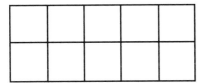

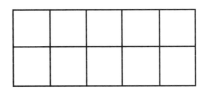

_____ + _____ = _____   _____ + _____ = _____

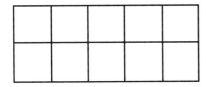

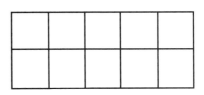

_____ + _____ = _____   _____ + _____ = _____

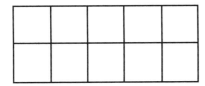

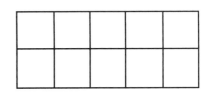

_____ + _____ = _____   _____ + _____ = _____

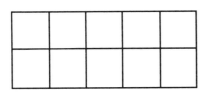

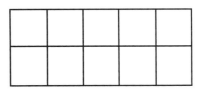

_____ + _____ = _____   _____ + _____ = _____

Mystery Sums, Version 1

Name: _____

Directions

1. Use your ten-frame cards to figure out what the mystery cards may be.

2. Record pictures or number sentences that match your thinking.

I'm holding three ten-frame cards and the sum of the cards is twelve. What might I be holding?

Mystery Sums, Version 2

Name: _____

Directions

1. Use your ten-frame cards to help you solve the problem.

2. Record as many solutions as you can find by writing number sentences that match the cards you used.

I am holding three mystery cards. The sum of my cards is fifteen. What cards might I be holding?

Mystery Sums Assessment Rubric

Use this rubric to determine a grade for the *Mystery Sums* assessment. Circle or check one box in each row.

Found no solutions. 10 points	Found 1–2 correct solutions. 15 points	Found 3–4 correct solutions. 20 points	Found 5 or more correct solutions. 25 points
Wrote none of the number sentences correctly. 10 points	Wrote less than half of the number sentences correctly. 15 points	Wrote more than half of the number sentences correctly. 20 points	Wrote all the number sentences correctly. 25 points
Was unable to use the ten-frame cards or blank ten-frame. 10 points	Used the ten-frame cards and blank ten-frame. 15 points	Used the ten-frame cards and didn't need the blank ten-frame. 20 points	Used mental math and didn't need the ten-frame cards or blank ten-frame. 25 points
Worked one-on-one with a teacher for the majority of the time. 10 points	Needed constant prompting and worked independently some of the time. 15 points	Needed a little prompting but mostly worked independently. 20 points	Needed no prompting; worked independently. 25 points

Partial Sums, Version 1

Name: _____

1. The second grade was selling pencils for a fund-raiser. One class sold 23 pencils and another class sold 34 pencils. How many pencils did the classes sell?

2. During recess, 42 students were playing outside. 25 more students joined them. How many students were playing outside?

3. Two classes went on a field trip to the zoo. One class had 24 students and the other class had 31 students. How many students went to the zoo?

4. During the field trip to the zoo, the students saw 21 birds and 15 snakes. How many birds and snakes did the students see?

5. While at the zoo the students also saw 27 penguins and 22 monkeys. How many penguins and monkeys did the students see?

Partial Sums, Version 2

Name: _____

1. Kobe bought a snack for 48 cents and a drink for 25 cents. How much money did Kobe spend?

2. Kylie was collecting stickers. She sorted them into two groups. One group had 27 stickers and the other group had 37 stickers. How many stickers does Kylie have?

3. During recess, the students were playing basketball. One team scored 45 points and the other team scored 25 points. How many points were scored by both teams?

4. At the school bake sale, Kylie bought a cookie for 33 cents and a brownie for 38 cents. How much money did Kylie spend at the bake sale?

5. During a nature hike, Kobe counted 39 birds and 23 squirrels. How many animals did Kobe count?

Partial Sums, Version 3

Name: _____

1. Jose had _____ cents in his wallet. His mom gave him _____ cents. How much money does Jose have?

2. The neighborhood had a block party. There were _____ hot dogs and _____ hamburgers. How many hot dogs and hamburgers were there altogether?

3. In the school garden there were _____ tulips and _____ sunflowers. How many flowers were in the school garden?

4. At the park, Kierra counted _____ ducks and _____ squirrels. How many ducks and squirrels did Kierra count?

5. Two classes were going on a field trip. One class had _____ students. The other class had _____ students. How many students are going on the field trip?

Ten-Frame

Note: Enlarge to create a demonstration version of the ten-frame.

Ten-Frame Cards

*Note: For the demonstration version of the ten-frame cards. A **complete set** of ten-frame cards is four copies of Reproducible B.*

(continued)

(Ten-Frame Cards, *continued*)

Ten-Frame Cards with Ten Dots

Note: Enlarge to create a demonstration version of the ten-frame cards with ten dots.

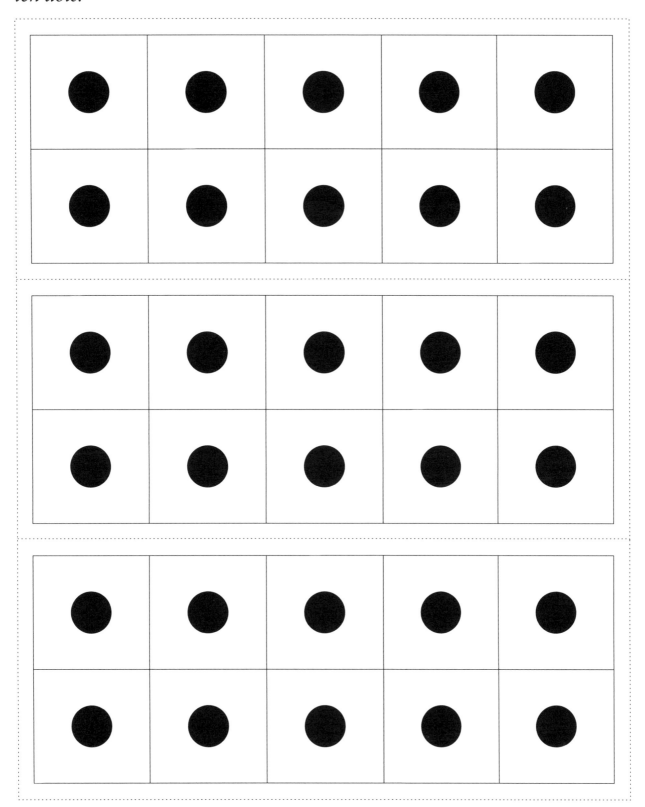

(continued)

Double Ten-Frame

Note: Enlarge to create a demonstration version of the double ten-frame.

Dot Cards

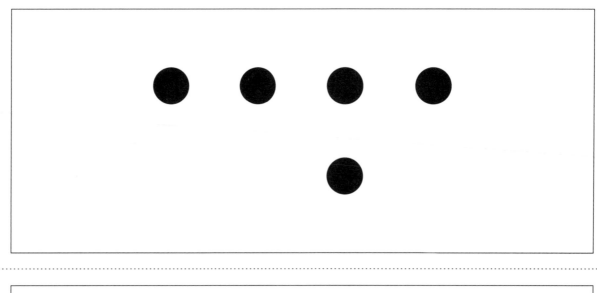

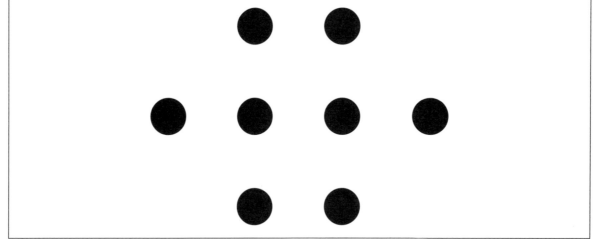

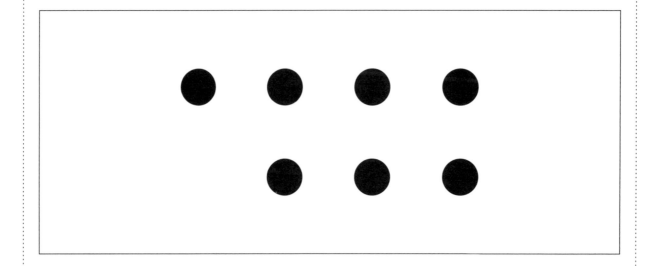

(continued)

(Dot Cards, *continued*)

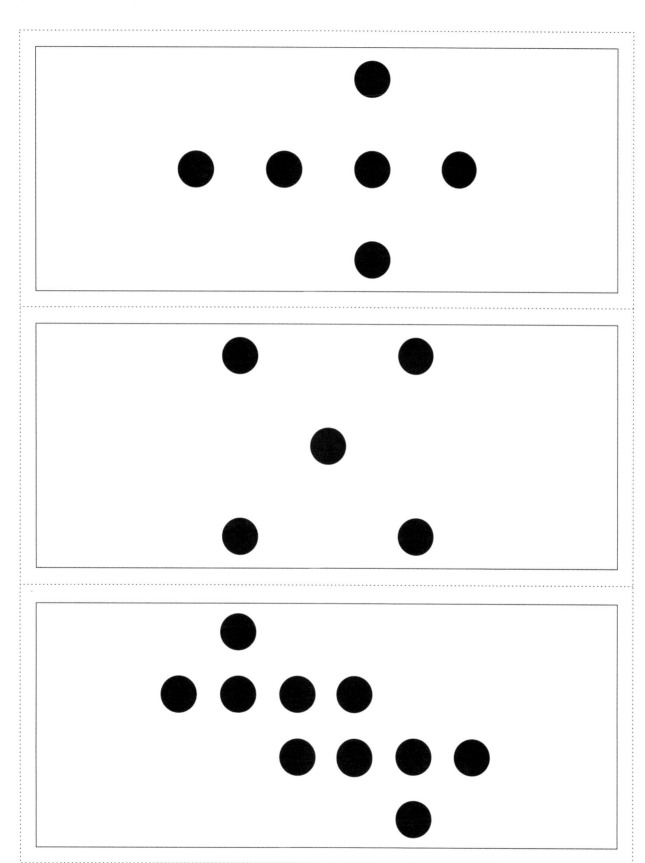

(*continued*)

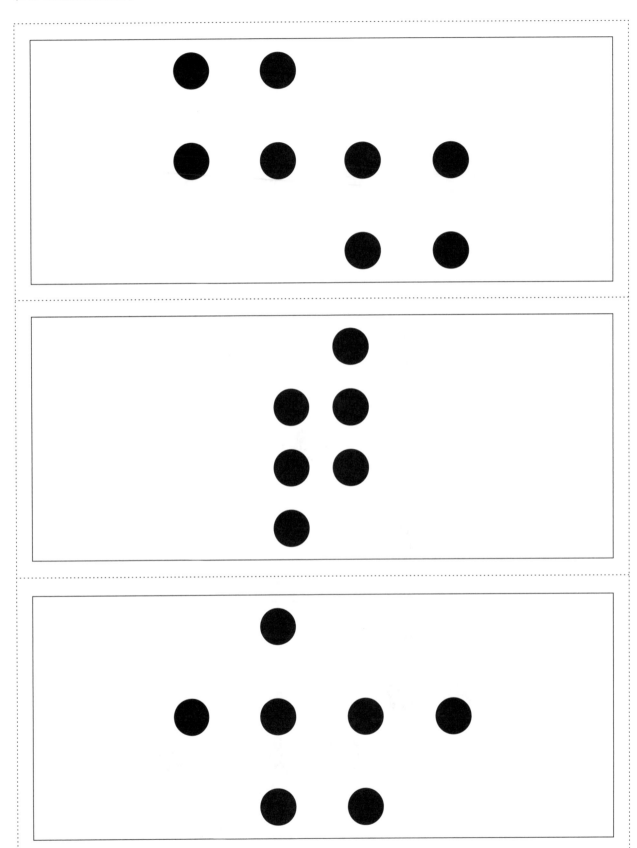

(*continued*)

(Dot Cards, *continued*)

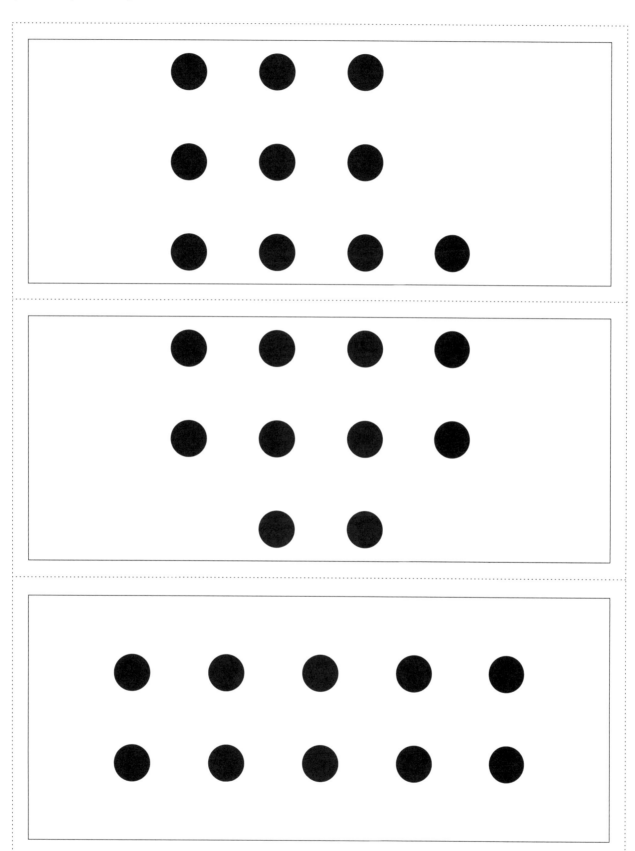

Numeral Cards

1

2

3

(continued)

4

5

6

7

8

9

(*continued*)

Computation Cards, Set A: Addition

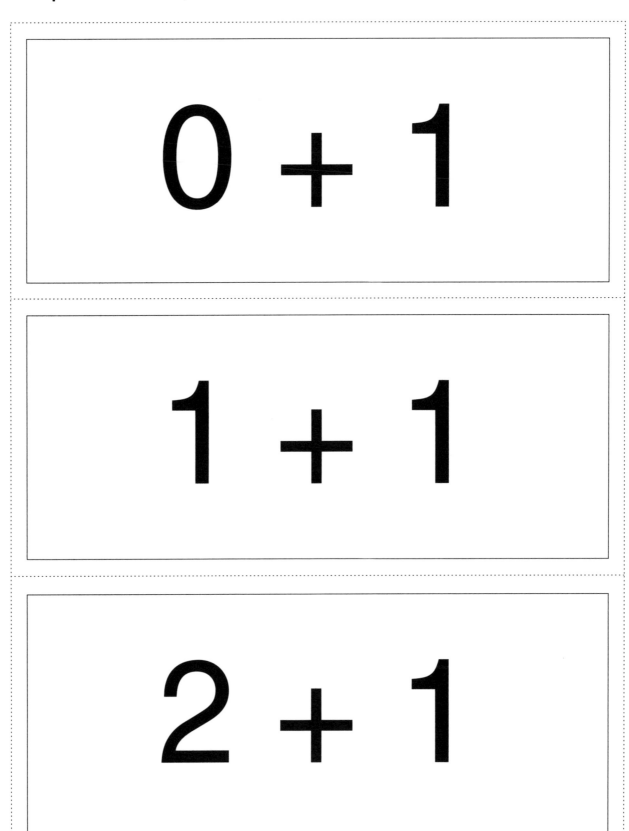

(continued)

$$2 + 2$$

$$3 + 2$$

$$3 + 3$$

(*continued*)

$$2 + 5$$

$$3 + 5$$

$$2 + 7$$

(continued)

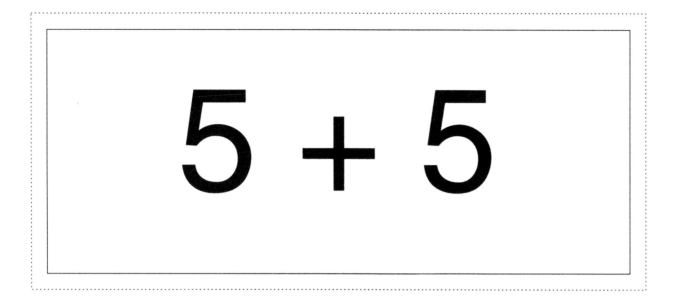

Computation Cards, Set B: Subtraction

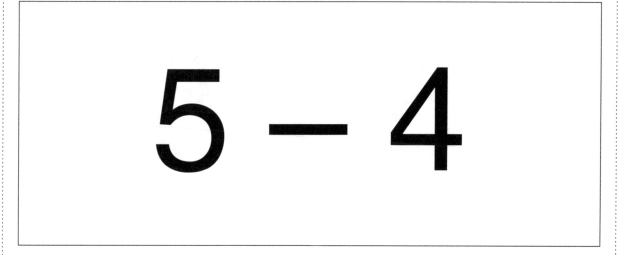

5 – 4

10 – 8

6 – 3

(continued)

9 − 5

15 − 10

8 − 2

(*continued*)

Computation Cards, Set C: Addition and Subtraction

$$6 - 5$$

$$4 - 2$$

$$2 + 1$$

(continued)

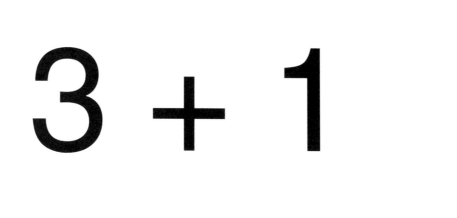

$$3 + 1$$

$$10 - 5$$

$$4 + 2$$

9 – 2

4 + 4

3 + 6

(continued)

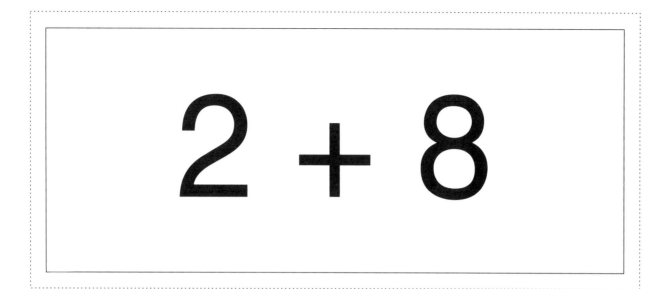

Hundreds Chart

1	2	3	4	5	6	7	8	9	10
11	12	13	14	15	16	17	18	19	20
21	22	23	24	25	26	27	28	29	30
31	32	33	34	35	36	37	38	39	40
41	42	43	44	45	46	47	48	49	50
51	52	53	54	55	56	57	58	59	60
61	62	63	64	65	66	67	68	69	70
71	72	73	74	75	76	77	78	79	80
81	82	83	84	85	86	87	88	89	90
91	92	93	94	95	96	97	98	99	100